ARCO

IN-A-FLASH VOCABULARY

for the SAT & ACT

Joan Carris

7th Edition

THOMSON ™

PETERSON'S

Australia • Canada • Mexico • Singapore • Spain • United Kingdom • United States

THOMSON ™

PETERSON'S

An ARCO Book

ARCO is a registered trademark of Thomson Learning, Inc., and is used herein under license by Thomson Peterson's.

About Thomson Peterson's

Thomson Peterson's (www.petersons.com) is a leading provider of education information and advice, with books and online resources focusing on education search, test preparation, and financial aid. Its Web site offers searchable databases and interactive tools for contacting educational institutions, online practice tests and instruction, and planning tools for securing financial aid. Thomson Peterson's serves 110 million education consumers annually.

Petersons.com/publishing

Check out our Web site at www.petersons.com/publishing to see if there are any revisions or corrections to the content of this book. We've made sure the information in this book is accurate and up-to-date; however, the content may have changed since the time of publication.

For more information, contact Thomson Peterson's, 2000 Lenox Drive, Lawrenceville, NJ 08648; 800-338-3282; or find us on the World Wide Web at www.petersons.com/about.

ISBN 0-7689-2231-3

Printed in Canada

10 9 8 7 6 5 4 3 2 1   08 07 06

Seventh Edition

CONTENTS

VITAL INFORMATION

This is not another boring introduction. The next few pages really DO contain vital information, just as the heading says.

DO YOU NEED TO PUMP UP YOUR VOCABULARY?

Most people would like a big, strong vocabulary for about a zillion reasons, only one of which is needing an impressive SAT or ACT score.

Remember that your language doesn't just say who you are, it *trumpets* who you are. Either you sound bright and well educated or you don't. You can't fool people—not for long anyway. There is no substitute for an educated vocabulary. Your language will shape your life; I absolutely guarantee it.

HONEST TALK ABOUT LEARNING

When you're very young, learning happens all the time, and you don't even have to think about it. One day you're popping those little bits of cereal into your mouth, and the next day you're saying "Cheerio, Cheerio!" and a proud parent is grinning from ear to ear. Nothing to it.

Well, you're older now, and the truth is that most learning involves work. The more complex the subject, the more work it's apt to take. **But vocabulary is one of the EASIER things to learn if you go about it the right way.** Isn't that a relief? Also, people remember what they enjoy studying. We tried to build a great deal of FUN into this book.

ANALYZE YOURSELF. HOW DO YOU LEARN?

Ask yourself these few questions. Then you can use the answers to make learning the words in this book easier.

■ *Do you learn better in the early morning?* What an awful thought. Still, half the world is like this.

■ *Do you learn better in the late afternoon?* In the evening? When are you too sleepy to work well?

■ *Do you learn better with music on or off?* Be careful here. Most of us learn well only when it's quiet.

■ *Do you need to write something down to learn it?* I would have flunked history if I hadn't highlighted lines in the textbook and written a full outline of all we studied.

■ *Do you need to hear something to remember it?* More than one third of us learn best through our ears.

■ *Do you feel better about studying if you have iced tea, Coke, or something else with caffeine* to keep you alert?

■ *Is learning more apt to happen if you work with a friend* or study group, or do you work best alone?

■ *Do you learn more efficiently if you say* "I'm going to do this assignment in 30 minutes, no matter what"?

Think about all these topics. Where and when and how do you do your very best learning? You need to know.

WHY LEARN THE WORDS IN THIS BOOK?

The words in this book are the *must know* words for the SAT and ACT. As an SAT/PSAT coach, I've been keeping records for more than twenty-five years of the words that stump kids over and over again. Those words are all here.

Why do the same words appear again and again in most SAT and ACT prep books and on tests similar to the SAT? Because these particular words really do the job. They are some of our most descriptive, specific adjectives—our most precise, active verbs—our information-packed nouns—yet none is overused or trite.

Words used all the time lose their punch. Let's take *sad*. Sara is sad about losing her boyfriend. Does that give you a vivid picture of Sara? No, and that's why we need *downcast, gloomy, sorrowful, disheartened, morose, anguished, wretched,* and all the others, each with its separate shades of meaning, so that we know EXACTLY how Sara feels.

WHO NEEDS THIS MANY WORDS?

You do, if you want to go to college or if you want to be thought of as an intelligent person. Remember that you must have a respectable vocabulary to be a good reader, and about 90 percent of college work depends on reading comprehension. Also, competence in writing is required in college and on the job, and *only* good readers are good writers. Since you need to be a good reader AND writer (let's add good speaker too), a bigger vocabulary is obviously the first requirement.

Remember, too, that your aim in talking and writing is to communicate, not in a general way but very specifically. Accurate communication requires a large supply of words. If your boss asks you to analyze progress on a project, he won't appreciate "It's going, like, kinda okay, you know?"

Even if you're a math major or a computer techie, you'll need to communicate your knowledge effectively and persuasively to other people. Einstein had to explain to others the significance of $E = mc^2$.

Enough! you're hollering. Okay, because even if I gave you a hundred reasons for learning these words, it would still boil down to the real reason: *lifestyle choice.* Strong language skills will get you the job, and therefore the lifestyle that you want. Lousy language skills will limit your choices alarmingly.

So, think . . . Where do you want to go in life and how will you get there? We agree that an educated vocabulary is the first step. Now, how can you get one with a minimum of agony?

HOW TO LEARN EVERY WORD IN THIS BOOK

First, fire up your determination. People who make things happen are determined people. Just wishing is never enough. If it were, you'd have a Porsche in your driveway.

Next, try what I'm suggesting here. Then, if it doesn't work, make your own plan for mastering these lists. We're talking about only 400 to 500 words, depending on how many synonyms you learn along the way.

1. Flip through the book to get a feel for each lesson. There are thirty lists of words, only twelve words each, plus two roots and their necessary words, for a total of sixteen words in each lesson. You'll know at least a couple on each list, so you'll actually be learning fourteen words at most. Every five lists, there's a review lesson to make sure you still know the words.

2. Try this Three-Day Miracle Plan for each lesson:

3

Day 1—Read each word, its definition, and the example sentences. Read all the way through, because often a story will lead you from one word to the next. Concentrate on any word that seems hard to remember. After studying the roots and their example words, do Memory Fix, the first practice with words in each lesson.

Day 2—Do the rest of the exercises. Write in this book. Highlight. Underline. Check any questions about pronunciation in a collegiate dictionary like *Webster's* or *Random House*.

Day 3—Self-quiz. Write the new words on a separate piece of paper with a definition or synonyms for each. If you know them all, rent a movie with friends to celebrate. Tomorrow you can begin a new list.

3. You'll need just a few minutes a day for three months to learn every word in this book on our Three-Day Miracle Plan. That's just one summer—or late summer and early fall. If you can work faster, do it. If you're a slow worker, it would be smarter to learn fewer words thoroughly, so that you have them for life, rather than trying to cram in all the words, retaining hardly any.

4. If you learn best in a group, form an SAT or ACT study group, with regular meeting times and assignments. Medical students do this to learn their most difficult subjects, and you can, too. Group learning is usually fun.

5. Read* . . . and read some more. Nothing helps people to learn words like seeing them in context over and over again. (People who love to read always think SAT critical reading sections are easy.) If you come across a word you don't know, ask someone who does, then *write the word and its definition in this book.* Or look up the unknown word in a dictionary.

Read magazines or newspapers that are well written, such as *Sports Illustrated, The New York Times,* the *Christian Science Monitor*, the *Boston Globe*, and the *Washington Post*.

Read books on topics you like. If it isn't pleasurable, you won't do it. Reading is supposed to be fun.

---

* Check out the titles on pp. 253–256. All of them are favorites with people your age. Enjoy!

6. Yes, use the dictionary. It's your friend, and you need to have a solid relationship. Get a pocket dictionary to carry with you. All bright people act this way. And, if you're technologically inclined, access an online dictionary.

7. Limit your TV time. Unless you're trying to beef up your total of 18,000+ murders seen by graduation (the average for all high schoolers), punch the little OFF button and let the boob tube rest. Its vocabulary *stops* at the sixth-grade level, remember?

8. Think about opposites. Antonyms are useful memory tools. *Night* has much more meaning when contrasted with *day*. If you know that *joyful* is the opposite of *morose*, you'll remember what *morose* means even though you use it less often.

9. Think about roots. The etymology (word history + root) of a word is a vital clue to its meaning. You know that a *hydr*ant dispenses *water*. So if you *hydr*ate a substance, you're adding water. An an*hydr*ous compound has no water . . . and so on. Knowing roots is the key to the meaning of 60 to 70 percent of English words. Every root you learn is a kind of verbal gold. A root like *duc/duct* (lead, guide) is the basis for more than 2,000 English words. *Gen* in *gen*tleman, *gen*esis, and in*gen*uous has spawned more than 50 words, all of them favorites with SAT question-makers. *The roots you absolutely must know are in this book, two solid-gold roots per lesson.*

10. How can you remember all the words? Make flashcards. If law and medical students do it, then we should pay attention. Smart people do what works. Ask parents and friends to quiz you with the flashcards. Carry them with you in your pocket or purse. You'll be astounded at what you can learn in a few odd minutes here or there.

11. Use memory aids to fix words in your mind. These are called *mnemonic devices*. Mne = *memory* as in a*mne*sia, a*mne*sty, and *mne*monics. (See what I mean about roots?) Draw a picture on your flashcards if it helps. Connect a person to a word. Make a silly sentence using the word you need to memorize. *Brusque Bob Baker barks at me.* Mnemonics work best when they're personal.

Another great memory aid is writing. The old schoolmarm trick of "Write it ten times" was a trick that worked. It still does.

Try all this, okay? If you're not learning words like crazy after a few weeks, devise methods that you like better. In other words, move through this book at your own pace, in your own way. You're acquiring an educated vocabulary to use the rest of your life. And while you're learning the new words, *use them!* That's the only way to keep them forever.

WHAT YOU ALREADY KNOW—A QUICK REVIEW

This *will* be quick because you already know these critical bits of vocabulary. Just whip through this review, and you'll feel much happier about your vocabulary. These are terribly helpful clues to thousands of English words that you need, and you *really do know them*. They've just been hanging around in the back of your mind, waiting for you to call on them.

The two lessons here will take only 30 minutes each—probably the best hour you'll spend all week! *You're going to be amazed* at what you already know that will boost your score on any test involving words.

LESSON A

How do smart people learn? They write information down, read what they've written, and say it out loud. They may repeat these three steps a few times, fixing the material in mind, and then they'll have it forever. So, get smart! Write these roots down, learn their definitions and those of the sample words, and you'll be taking a large step toward a bigger vocabulary.

AQUA and **HYDR** = water and **MAR** = sea, ocean

aquarium	hydrant	marine
aqualung	hydraulic	aquamarine
aquamarine	dehydrate	mariner
aqueduct	hydrolysis	maritime
	hydrogen	submarine

So *aquamarine* (a pale turquoise-colored stone) really means "water of the sea," a perfect description.

EGO and **AUTO** = I, self

ego	autocrat
egotist	autograph
superego	automobile
egocentric	autobiography
alter ego	autonomous
	autodidactic

BIO = life
biology biopsy biography autobiography symbiosis

MATER = mother and **PATER = father**

matron	paternal
maternal	patriot
matrimony	paternity
matriarchal	patriarchal
maternity	patrimony

A *patriot*, therefore, is loyal to his *father*land.

AUD/AUDIT = hear
audition audible auditorium inaudible audience audit

SCRIB/SCRIPT and **GRAPH/GRAM = to write**

scribe	graphic
scribble	telegraph
inscribe	biography
describe	photography
prescribe	telegram
proscribe	mammogram
inscription	cardiogram
description	

My *auto-bio-graphy*, the story of my life, is literally "writing my life." Three roots in one word.

GE/GEO = earth and **AGR = field, soil**

geology	agriculture
geophysics	agronomy
geometry	agrarian
apogee	agrochemical

SCI and **COGN/COGNI/GNO(S) = to know**

science	cognizant
omniscient	cognate
prescient	incognito
conscious	recognize
	prognosis
	agnostic

Prescient . . . a tough word, right? Not anymore. The prefix *pre* meaning "before" and the root *sci* give you the meaning. *Prescient* means "knowing ahead of time, able to foretell."

VID/VIS = to see
video evident provide vision revise advise improvise

CHRON and **TEMPOR** = time

chronology	tempo
synchronize	temporize
chronometer	temporary
anachronism	contemporary
	extemporaneous

SENS/SENT = to feel

sensible resent dissent consent sensual presentiment

A *presentiment* is "a foreboding," a "feeling before" something happens that you know what's about to happen. Another gift from the world of roots!

CIV = citizen

civic civil civilian civilization civility

FALL/FALS = to deceive, be not truthful

fallacy fallacious infallible false falsify falsehood

Words from this root are *always* on the SAT and ACT!

CYCL = circle

cycle recycle cyclical tricycle bicycle Cyclops

NEG = to deny, not

negative renege renegade abnegation

And remember these incredibly useful prefixes? Read each one aloud slowly as a memory refresher.

A/AN = not, without

anomaly	atrophy
amoral	agnostic
atheist	anonymous
amorphous	atypical

AB/ABS = from, away

absent	abhor
abstain	abrupt
abbreviate	abrasive
abdicate	abnormal

(You knew you wanted to stay *away* from someone who was acting *ab*normal, right?)

AC/AD/AF, etc. = to, toward, against
adhere aggregate addict apportion aspect attend

ANTE/ANTI = before, previous

anteroom	anticipate	antedate
antecedent	antebellum	anterior

ANTI = against, opposing

antisocial	antithesis	antidote
antiseptic	antipathy	antibiotic

BENE = good, well

benefit	beneficial
beneficent	benefactor
benediction	benevolent

CIRCU = around

circuit	circuitous
circumspect	circumnavigate
circumvent	circumference

CO/COL/COM, etc. = with, together

collateral	cooperate	concede
coerce	collaborate	compassion
correlate	concur	

CONTRA/COUNTER = against, opposing

contradict	counteract	countereffective
contraband	contrary	

DI/DIA = across, apart, through, between

dilate	diaphragm
diameter	diaphanous
dialogue	dialectic

DIS/DI/DIFF = away, apart, negative

disparate	difference
diffuse	dissuade
disseminate	disperse

EN/EM = in, among, within

enliven	empathy	enhance
embarrass	embed	enforce

MEMORY CHECK Answers on page 241

To fix these important prefixes in your memory, fill in the missing info in this chart.

PREFIX	MEANING	EXAMPLES
A/An		atheist, anomaly, atypical
	from, away	
DIS/DI/DIFF		
	before, previous	anteroom, anticipate
BENE		
	around	
		diameter, dialogue, dilate
ANTI		
	against, opposing	
CO/COL/COM		cooperate, concede, concur

LESSON B

. . . because you can never know too many prefixes!

EPI = outside, over, outer
epilogue epidermis epitaph epiphany epicenter

EX/EXTRA/EXTER/EXTRO = out, outside, beyond
expel extrovert external extol extraordinary

HETERO = other
heterodox   heterogeneous   heterosexual

HOMO = same
homogeneous   homophone   homosexual
homonym

IN/IL/IM/IR = in, within or not, opposing

internal	imply	indecent
intrinsic	imprint	inefficient
influx	irradiate	illegal
irreverent		

11

INTER = among, between
interact   intervene   interdict   intersect

INTRA/INTRO = inwardly, within
intramural   intravenous   introduce   introvert

A small cheer here for roots and prefixes. One who turns (*vert*) himself *out* for others (an outgoing personality) is an *extro*vert; the *intro*vert is turned *in*ward (may be an *intro*spective type), a less open individual by far.

MACRO/MAG/MEGA/MAX = big, long
macrocosm   macroeconomics
magnitude   magnanimous
maximum   megalomaniac

MAL = bad, badly
malady   malicious   malign
malevolent maleficent   malinger
dismal   malaise

META/MET = change of, over, beyond
metaphor   metabolism
metaphysics   metamorphism
metastasize

MEMORY CHECK 1   Answers on page 241

Try your hand at completing the following sentences.

1 The elephant wears his *epi*dermis on the

_____.

2 A *hetero*geneous group is

_____.

3 A naked ghost would be both _____decent *and* _____substantial, right?

4 Playing it to the *max* means

_____.

5 We know *Male*ficent means trouble in "Sleeping Beauty" because she has such a

_____ name.

6 Our favorite *meta*morphic critter is the butterfly, who _____ his form (*morph*) into one that can fly.

MICRO = small

microbe   microscope   microphone   microcosm

OMNI and PAN = all, entire

omnivorous	panorama
omnipresent	panacea
omniscient	pandemic
	pandemonium
	pantheon

ORTH = straight, right

orthodox   orthodontist   orthopedic   orthotics

PAR/PARA = beside, next to

paradox	paragon
parenthesis	paraphrase
paradigm	parasite

PER = through, throughout or completely, wrongly

persecute	permeate
perjury	permit
perturb	persiflage

PERI = around, near

perimeter   periscope   peripatetic   periphery

POST = after, following

postpone   posthumous   postmortem   posterior

PRE = before

predict	prefix
preordained	preliminary
pregnant	precipitate
precocious	predilection

PRO = for, forward, before, forth, favoring

progress	promote
progenitor	prognosis
provision	promise

RE/RETRO = back, again

recoil	retreat
retain	retroactive
retrospect	recur
refer	rehearse
reiterate	remember

MEMORY CHECK 2 Answers on page 241

As before, fill in the missing boxes in the chart.

PREFIX	MEANING	EXAMPLES
	small	microbe, microphone, microcosm
PRE		predict, prefix, preliminary
	straight, right	
PER		permeate, permit
	around, near	periscope, perimeter, periphery
PRO		
	after, following	
		recoil, retreat, retroactive
OMNI, PAN		

SE = apart, away from

seclude	segregate
secede	sequester
seduce	separate

14

SUB/SUC/SUF/SUG/SUM/SUP/SUS = under, below

subzero	submarine
succeed	suffuse
suggest	summon
suppose	suspend

SUPER/SUR = over, above, extra

superstar	superimpose
survey	surpass
superficial	surmount

SYL/SYM/SYN/SYS = together

syllable	symmetry
symphony	synergy
synopsis	synthesis
system	systolic

TELE = from afar

telegram   telephone   telephoto   telescope   telemetry

TRA/TRANS = across, beyond

traverse	travesty
trajectory	transport
transgress	transform

UN and IN = not, opposing

unwary	unequal
unmitigated	unsuspecting
indistinct	inequitable

WITH = against

withhold   withstand   withdraw

15

MEMORY CHECK 3 Answers on page 241

> **Fill in the blanks in the following sentences.**

1 If you *se*clude a criminal in order to *se*gregate him from society, you have _____ him from normal life.

2 A *tele*phone brings you voices from _____.

3 That long, cigar-shaped ship that stays "under the sea" for months at a time is rightly called a _____.

4 A _____ store will provide _____ savings that will _____pass your wildest dreams. These stores truly are *over* and *above* all others, offering many *extras*.

5 The purpose of _____chronizing our watches is so that we will be _____ in time (*chron*).

LIST OF ABBREVIATIONS

Take a minute to familiarize yourself with the following abbreviations, which are used in the vocabulary lessons.

n.	noun	**s.**	singular	**L.**	Latin
v.	verb	**pl.**	plural	**Fr.**	French
adj.	adjective	**usu.**	usually	**Sp.**	Spanish
adv.	adverb	**lit.**	literally	**Gr.**	Greek
				Ger.	Germanic

LIST 1

A LAUDABLE LIST OF VERBS

acquiesce • chastise • augment • condone •
amass • disseminate • coalesce • concur •
digress • laud • disperse • efface

ACQUIESCE v. *to give in and agree peaceably; to assent, comply* n. **acquiescence**
When Dad set 1 a.m. as our curfew, my sister Amy and I *acquiesced* because we knew he meant business. For me, it's easier to *acquiesce* than to argue forever, which I hate.

CHASTISE v. *to scold severly or punish; castigate, censure*
Every day we *chastise* Dude, my insanely brave, five-pound Yorkshire terrier. But Meatloaf, Amy's 16-pound cat, has almost never been *chastised*, probably because she's too smart to get caught.

AUGMENT v. *to increase; to make something greater or bigger*
Dad said, "Ted, I'll *augment* your allowance for your senior year, in return for more help at home." That could mean major labor, but I have to *augment* my savings before college.

CONDONE v. *to overlook or pardon an offense; to excuse*
For too long, our family has *condoned* Dude's mad-dog tendencies. We keep making excuses for him, unlike my high school principal, who rarely *condones* misbehavior.

AMASS v. *to accumulate, collect; to gather, come together*
I don't need to *amass* a huge fortune, but a bit of extra money would be nice—for camping gear, of course. Whenever ours is *amassed* in one place, I see how much we need.

DISSEMINATE v. *to disperse or spread everywhere (knowledge or ideas) as if sowing seeds*

Our school paper, *The Central Times*, tries to *disseminate* the information all students need. As editor, I hope the paper also *disseminates* the spirit of Central High.

COALESCE v. *to mix or come together from separate elements*

Thoughts about my last editorial finally *coalesced* into one good idea. Amy couldn't believe I was actually writing about her play cast, a group of radically different kids that I saw *coalescing* into a supportive stage family.

CONCUR v. *to agree, assent; to approve; to coincide*

After much discussion, our family *concurred* on a camping site for next summer. Luckily, Dad's vacation time is *concurrent* with the best time to visit the park we selected.

DIGRESS v. *to wander off course in speaking or writing*

I often *digress* into related topics as I get into a speech. I think these *digressions* are humorous, but my teacher has started saying, "Ted, if you keep *digressing*, I'll mark you down. You must stay on target."

LAUD v. *to praise, commend, acclaim, extol*

We rarely say, "You are to be *lauded* for that achievement" anymore, favoring the word praised or commended instead. But I often hear "What a *laudable* accomplishment."

DISPERSE v. *to spread all over; to disseminate;* also, *to fan out or scatter in a random way*

With promotion of school events as one goal, we *disperse* copies of *The Central Times* to each class. Most kids came to the recent basketball tournament and *dispersed* like so many bats afterward, flitting home to study for exams.

MISS/MIT = to send

emit—*to voice; to give off, as fumes or anger*
　　　emitted a low groan
　　　emit foul fumes
　　　emission standards

mission—*a definite job or task; the mission establishment itself (usually religious)*
　　　needing a clear *mission*
　　　the old adobe Jesuit *mission*

Also: **omit, omission, commit, commission, permit, permission, transmit, transmission, missive, missile**

EFFACE v. *to erase or obliterate; to wear away (as by time)*
I'm counting on time to *efface* the memories of when I've made a total idiot of myself, just as weather has gradually *effaced* the harsh or exaggerated features of nature.

MEMORY FIX

To learn these new words, write each one on a sheet of paper. Also write a synonym or definition for each and say the words aloud as you work.

FILL IN THE BLANKS Answers on page 242

> Using the words in List 1, select the one that best completes the meaning and logic of each phrase below. Note which tense or form of the word is required for sense.

1 wouldn't _____ unless I could yield with a clear conscience

2 can't possibly _____ that rude behavior

3 harsh weather that _____ the writing on the tomb

4 formal enough to say _____ instead of scold

5 an opinion that fortunately _____ with mine

6 "all glory, _____, and honor" goes the hymn

7 to _____ as much as possible, the goal of Scrooge McDuck

8 eager to _____ the number of qualified students

9 careful to focus on the problem and not _____

10 a thorough reading, please, not a _____ one

11 a rambling, _____ talk that put everyone to sleep

12 where the two paths _____ into one wider path

13 hope to _____ the news to as many as possible

14 quit milling around and _____ peaceably now

15 _____ a low cry of astonishment before falling silent

ANALOGIES   Answers on page 242

> Choose the one word pair in each list below that expresses the same relationship as the pair in capital letters.

1 CHASTISE : MISBEHAVIOR

(A) start : argument
(B) castigate : students
(C) laud : success
(D) represent : hope
(E) remunerate : reward

2 FOOTPRINTS : EFFACE

(A) scars : hide
(B) gulley : widen
(C) target : omit
(D) memorial : dedicate
(E) record : obliterate

3 ACQUIESCE : YIELDING

(A) comply : hesitating
(B) disperse : scattering
(C) concur : running
(D) emit : smelling
(E) commit : halting

4 PATH : STRAY

(A) lecture : digress
(B) book : review
(C) illness : recur
(D) duties : remiss
(E) elements : coalesce

5 PARDON : OFFENSE

   (A) amass : wealth
   (B) punish : wrongdoing
   (C) condone : error
   (D) censure : actions
   (E) disseminate : cheer

MATCHING Answers on page 242

> **Choose the two words or phrases that best explain the meaning of each of the words in bold type.**

1 acquiesce

   (A) dispute
   (B) assent
   (C) drench
   (D) yield

2 emit

   (A) utter
   (B) voice
   (C) take in
   (D) abhor

3 castigate

   (A) scorn
   (B) chastise
   (C) scold
   (D) tie up

4 precursor

   (A) forerunner
   (B) patron
   (C) arbiter
   (D) harbinger

5 amass

   (A) ritual
   (B) accumulate
   (C) gather
   (D) Southern for "disaster"

6 augment

   (A) enlarge
   (B) add to
   (C) alter
   (D) price

7 **disperse**

(A) avoid
(B) strew around
(C) arrange
(D) disseminate

8 **coalesce**

(A) join
(B) roil around
(C) come together
(D) disturb

9 **efface**

(A) embarrass
(B) wear away
(C) erase
(D) expose

10 **cursory**

(A) sketchy
(B) cautious
(C) ignorant
(D) hasty

2 DOWN WITH BOMBAST!

banal • terse • raconteur • euphemism • succinct • hackneyed • bombast • articulate • laconic • hyperbole • lampoon • platitude

BANAL adj. *commonplace and stale, not fresh; trite, insipid* n. **banality**
Banal, overused phrases and words are so numerous that it's hard to avoid them. Those of us who work on the *Times* cut these *banalities* from every article, including our own, because *banal* means boring, every time.

TERSE adj. *stripped of all but the essentials; concise or succinct, sometimes to the point of rudeness*
When you need encouragement, a *terse* response is disappointing. For instance, that small, *terse* "B" on my history paper seemed like a stingy response to my weeks of research.

RACONTEUR n. *gifted talker or storyteller*
My English lit class read *The Importance of Being Earnest* by Oscar Wilde, a talented playwright, poet, and *raconteur* who, because he was so amusing, was an extremely popular guest. Wilde died in poverty in Paris; when a friend offered him champagne on his deathbed, Wilde remarked, "I am dying beyond my means."

EUPHEMISM n. *the use of a "nice" word or phrase instead of an offensive or terrible honest one; the word or phrase so used*
My last editorial was on the *euphemism* "ethnic cleansing," a phrase used to disguise the murders in Bosnia-Herzegovina and Rwanda. I enjoy some common *euphemisms*, such as "precocious" (spoiled brat) or "made redundant" ("fired" in Britain), but using a *euphemism* to cloak genocide is revolting.

SUCCINCT adj. *brief, to the point; concise, pithy, terse*
Some critics favor the taut, *succinct* writing style of Hemingway or Cather. I enjoy a more colloquial style,

like Mark Twain's in *Huckleberry Finn*. For the school paper, of course, we demand *succinct*, pithy articles.

HACKNEYED adj. *banal, overused, commonplace, trite*
The *hackney* was a breed of horse used to pull the old public coaches in England. From their regular, boring routine came the words *hackneyed* and *hack*.

BOMBAST n. *high-flown, pompous, "windbag" language*
The windy, *bombastic* mayor of our town likes to give speeches. Whenever he comes to school, this Bard of *Bombast* yaks away, one empty paragraph after another.

ARTICULATE v. *to speak in a clear, effective way* adj. *clear and effective in manner;* also, *jointed or marked off (as "the beetle's* articulated *segments")*
Amy practices a lot, trying to *articulate* her lines perfectly. I admit that she's a really *articulate* performer, but life with an actress is hard to take.

LOC/LOQU/LOG/OLOGY = speech, study, word, talk

eloquent—*extremely expressive (a gesture or words)*
    a moving, *eloquent* speech
    the *eloquent* bowing of his head

loquacious—*extremely talkative; gabby, garrulous*
    a *loquacious* parrot
    the *loquaciousness* born of loneliness

Also: **elocution, soliloquy, colloquial, prologue, epilogue, tautology** (*redundancy*)**, eulogy, psychology, biology**

VOC/VOK = to call

vociferous—*loudly, persistently vocal; clamorous*
    the *vociferous* wail of a hungry baby
    a *vociferous* message

equivocal—*open to two interpretations, evasive, unclear*
    a puzzling, *equivocal* answer
    an *equivocal*, uneasy reply

Also: **provoke, provocative, vocal, equivocate, evoke, evocative, invoke, invocation, revoke**

25

LACONIC adj. *using as few words as possible; concise*

The old Greek Spartans from the area Laconia were big-deed-doers, not talkers, and came to be known as *laconic* folk. The most *laconic* communication I've heard of was between Victor Hugo, author of *Les Miserables*, and his publisher. After the book came out, Hugo wrote: ? His publisher replied: !

HYPERBOLE n. *wild exaggeration, often on purpose for effect*

Reading Twain is fun, partly because he uses *hyperbole* so well. So does the cast on *Saturday Night Live*. The crazy exaggeration of *hyperbole* is probably as much fun for the actors as it is for their audience.

LAMPOON n. *verbal ridicule of a person; personal satire* v. **to ridicule**

The cast of *Saturday Night Live* loves to *lampoon* political figures, especially the president. They let their *lampooning* go as far as TV standards allow.

PLATITUDE n. *a tired, trite old saying; a banality*

Remember our bombastic mayor? Well, one reason he's so boring is that he just mouths *platitudes*, like all windbags, and everybody's tired of hearing the same old sayings. *Platitudes* put people to sleep.

MEMORY FIX

To learn these new words, write each one on a sheet of paper. Also write a synonym or definition for each and say the new words aloud as you work.

TRUE OR FALSE   Answers on page 242

> **Read each sentence below to see how each word in List 2 is being used. Then mark T (true) or F (false) beside each.**

1 You wouldn't enjoy a *raconteur* at your party.

_____

2 We have many *euphemisms* for the word "died."

_____

3 Hugh's repertoire of *hackneyed* jokes makes us roar with laughter. _____

4 A *laconic* speech is sure to drag on forever. _____

5 If I ask for a *terse* report, I mean a *succinct* one. _____

6 We sat spellbound and attentive as the speaker uttered one *platitude* after another. _____

7 *Hyperbole* is often used to good effect in a *lampoon*. _____

8 A person with a fine mind probably created this *banal* essay. _____

9 A pompous, self-important person is apt to deliver a *bombastic* speech. _____

10 The more *articulate* you are, the greater our chance of understanding your message. _____

MATCHING   Answers on page 242

> **Match the words in column A with their meanings in column B.**

	A	B
_____	**1.** eloquent	**a.** garrulous
_____	**2.** banality	**b.** great exaggeration
_____	**3.** vociferous	**c.** to say effectively
_____	**4.** trite	**d.** moving and expressive
_____	**5.** tautology	**e.** pompous
_____	**6.** articulate (v.)	**f.** evasive

_____ 7. bombastic   **g.** platitude

_____ 8. provoke   **h.** hackneyed

_____ 9. loquacious   **i.** redundancy

_____ 10. laconic   **j.** sparing of speech

_____ 11. hyperbole   **k.** to arouse or spark

_____ 12. equivocal   **l.** insistent and loud

FILL IN THE BLANKS   Answers on page 242

> **Using the words in List 2, select the ones that best complete the meaning and logic of each sentence.**

1 An editor who complains that your book lacks originality is saying that it is

b_____ and

h_____.

2 Five words that refer to the extremely economical use of language are **c**_____,

s_____,

l_____,

t_____, and

p_____.

3 "Mile-high pie" is an example of

_____.

4 A **p**_____ is stale and overused, a trite remark, just like a

b_____.

5 The opposite of a clearcut answer is a(n)

_____ one.

SYCOPHANTS HAVE BROWN NOSES

despot • sycophant • glutton • hedonist • hypocrite • heretic • charlatan • bigot • miser • insurgent • zealot • skeptic

DESPOT n. *a ruler with total control; a tyrant, autocrat*
My 5-pound Yorky, sees himself as king of our house, a real *despot* with all of us under his paw. Amy's cat, Meatloaf, never yields to doggy *despotism*, of course.

SYCOPHANT n. *a brownnoser; one who flatters others; a toady*
Kids dislike *sycophants* because their brownnosing is so hypocritical. Powerful people must enjoy that servile flattery or we wouldn't have so many *sycophants*.

GLUTTON n. *one who is overly, almost sinfully, hungry for something, usually food* n. **glut** v. **to glut**
Amy's a *glutton* for roles on stage. "I'll play any part," she says. Recently, wrapped in thick padding, she portrayed *Gluttony* itself in a Christian morality play about the seven deadly sins.

HEDONIST n. *someone who lives for pleasure or happiness*
In class we discussed the Greek doctrine of *hedonism*, which held that happiness or pleasure was the sole good in life. We contrasted the *hedonist's* pleasure-seeking goals with the Puritan's spiritual, work-oriented life, and ended up voting for a blend of the two—the old Greek "golden mean."

HYPOCRITE n. *one who pretends to a life or beliefs that he doesn't honestly have; a phony or fake*
The guys I know don't admire a *hypocrite* or *hypocrisy* of any kind. It's so phony. Think about tennis star Arthur Ashe, who was always honest and straightforward, never phony. "Not a *hypocritical* bone in him," my friend Jason says.

ORA = to speak, pray

inexorable—*not movable by any means; inflexible, relentless*

> *inexorable* hand of fate
> the *inexorable* march of time

oracle—*one who gives wise or especially meaningful advice*

> Greek *oracle* at Delphi
> the principal, our school's *oracle*

Also: **oracular, orator, peroration** *(a long, grandiose speech)*

HERETIC n. *one who differs from accepted belief or theory*

"Would you guys hang me as a *heretic* if I suggested eliminating the Social Corner?" I asked the newspaper staff. They agreed to cut the column and admitted that occasionally *heretics* have good ideas. (But often the mere suspicion of *heresy* is fatal. Witches were burned as *heretics* by fanatics, remember?)

CHARLATAN n. *a quack or fraud; a cheat, imposter*

My dad's office is just recovering from being cheated by a master *charlatan* who posed as a management consultant. The real skill of *charlatans* is lying, apparently.

BIGOT n. *one who stubbornly holds to his own opinions*

VER = truth

verify—*to establish truth or accuracy; to confirm*

> *verify* his whereabouts
> try to *verify* his statement

aver—*to state firmly and convincingly; declare positively*

> "For all *averred*, I had killed the bird
> That made the breeze to blow.
> Ah wretch! said they, the bird to slay,
> That made the breeze to blow!"
>
> *The Rime of the Ancient Mariner*, Samuel Taylor Coleridge

Also: **verdict, verisimilitude, veracious** *(truthful)*

I hope age doesn't turn me into a narrow-minded *bigot* like some I know. I hate prejudice, and *bigoted* people are usually very opinionated.

MISER n. *a greedy, grasping person (L. miser = miserable)*
One of my friends is really a *miser*, in contrast to the rest of us, who are mainly generous guys. We tease him about being a *miserly* Scrooge type, but his stinginess is less amusing as time goes by.

INSURGENT n. *a rebel; one who rises up in revolt*
As an editor I need to study newspapers, so I'm always aware of *insurgent* forces in other countries. My sympathies are with *insurgents* whenever they're revolting against a cruel political regime, as in Haiti.

ZEALOT n. *a fanatic; someone devoted beyond reason to a cause or belief*

As the self-appointed defender of the family, Dude is our personal *zealot*. Daily he patrols our property, barking *zealously* whenever a stranger threatens to cross over into his territory.

SKEPTIC n. *one who doubts or waits to pass judgment*
Thomas Huxley, the famous English biologist, knew that a good scientist was a *skeptic*. He said, "Skepticism is the highest of duties, blind faith the one unpardonable sin." A *skeptic* is the opposite of a zealot or fanatic.

MEMORY FIX
To learn these new words, write each one on a sheet of paper. Also write a synonym or definition for each and say the words aloud as you work.

FILL IN THE BLANKS   Answers on page 243

Using the words in List 3, select the one that best
completes the meaning and logic of each phrase.
Note which tense or form of the word is required
for sense.

1 dangerous crew of armed
_____ spearheading the revolt

2 the _____ habit of saying one
thing while thinking another

3 needs one _____ week just
having fun this summer

4 a true workaholic, a regular
_____ for more challenges

5 as _____ as the cycle of the
seasons

6 those practiced _____ who
skillfully deceive us

7 looked like a real diamond, but I was still
_____

8 a strong autocrat, but even so a benevolent
_____

9 the _____ in our midst,
determined to go against established tradition

10 suffering from an excess of zeal, a
_____ for sure

11 hoarding his candy like a

_____ hoards his wealth

12 the most _____, prejudiced

person I ever met

13 the servile behavior of a known

_____

14 necessary that you _____ the

accuracy of this report

RHYME TIME Answers on page 243

Complete these couplets of pretty awful poetry (PAP) with the correct form of one of this list's new words or an important synonym.

1 Said Orson Welles, whose size doubled by twice,

"_____ is not a secret vice."

2 We keep loony Aunt Tilly up in the attic,

'Cause everyone knows she's a raving

_____.

3 When I need advice on a matter historical,

I ask my teacher, the school's living

_____.

4 A _____ says, "I was born to doubt,

Until the facts of the matter come out."

5 We couldn't believe he gave her that plant,

But he's a toady, you know, a

_____.

6 "Lookin' for fun in all the right places,"

Sings the _____ eager for

bright party faces.

7 Nature's _____ laws we spurn,

Only if we're too dimwitted to learn.

8 I was quick to _____ when I

testified that Hugo would never run off or hide.

MATCHING Answers on page 243

In column B, find two synonyms or phrases to explain each word in column A, and write their letters on the correct lines.

	A	B	
_____	1. miser	**a.** bias	**i.** fake, fraud
_____	2. heretic	**b.** corroborate	**j.** one in revolt
_____	3. despot	**c.** hoarder	**k.** prejudice
_____	4. charlatan	**d.** nonbeliever	**l.** fanatical
_____	5. bigotry	**e.** rebel	**m.** Scrooge
_____	6. verify	**f.** tyrant	**n.** overeager
_____	7. zealous	**g.** imposter	**o.** confirm
_____	8. insurgent	**h.** autocrat	**p.** one who differs

HOW GERMANE, MY DEAR

fervent • germane • fortuitous • grueling • indulgent • vulnerable • profuse • superficial • uniform • listless • incessant • unobtrusive

FERVENT adj. *full of strong emotion; impassioned*
Meatloaf vents her anger in *fervent* yowls when another cat invades our yard. The *fervor* of Meatloaf's response to feline trespassers seems much louder at night, when we *fervently* wish she'd shut up.

GERMANE adj. *fitting and appropriate; relevant; pertinent*
The Mark Twain quotes I like best aren't *germane* to my talk, so I can't use them. Our speech teacher always says, "Omit the extras and concentrate on the *germane* material when giving a brief talk."

FORTUITOUS adj. *happening by chance; accidental*
Meatloaf stalks mice deliberately, but she also has her share of *fortuitous* meetings. Happening upon a mouse is *fortuitous* not only for Meatloaf but also for the mouse, who would never have planned to meet a cat.

GRUELING adj. *demanding and exhausting; punishing, tiring*
In one *grueling* day, the newspaper staff washed over 400 cars to raise money for a new computer. At home later, exhausted but proud, I told the folks just how *grueling* a task it had been.

INDULGENT adj. *generous to a fault; lenient, not critical*
We've been too *indulgent* with Dude, and so he's badly spoiled. We've agreed to stop *indulging* him right now. As Shakespeare warned us, an *indulgent* person loves "not wisely but too well."

> ### CLAUS/CLUD/CLUS = close, shut
>
> **preclude**—*to forestall, hinder, avert, or prevent*
> the storm *precluded* our hike
> that rule *precludes* his joining
>
> **recluse**—*a hermit; one living a solitary life*
> a wealthy, eccentric *recluse*
> his withdrawn, *reclusive* life
>
> Also: **exclude, exclusion, claustrophobia, include, inclusion**

VULNERABLE adj. *open to physical or mental damage or hurt*

Unaware of the word *vulnerable* as a kid, I still knew the feeling of being open to attack from mean guys on the playground at recess. When you're *vulnerable*, you know you're without a good defense.

PROFUSE adj. *in great abundance; bountiful; lavish; lush*

The phrase "*profuse* apologies" describes a gushing flood of "I'm sorrys." During a tough wrestling match, my *profuse* perspiration is another kind of flood.

Unfortunately, our county has a *profusion* of great high school wrestlers.

SUPERFICIAL adj. *on the surface, shallow; not deep, serious, or important; cursory, not thorough*

I got some *superficial* cuts from cleats in the last soccer game; fortunately, *superficial* wounds normally heal without causing trouble. In contrast, a *superficial* judgment is apt to cause lots of trouble.

UNIFORM adj. *consistent (as opposed to varied); the same*

I think *uniformity* of design, as in a row of identical houses or apartments, is boring. But at school I want consistency and fairness—*uniform* attendance policies and *uniform* grading systems.

LISTLESS adj. *lacking energy or enthusiasm; indifferent or languid; uncaring*

When we found Meatloaf staring at her food with dull, *listless* eyes, we knew she was sick. Any *listlessness* toward dinner on that cat's part is serious. When I had the flu, I remember feeling *listless* toward everything.

36

> **POT/POSS = to be powerful or able**
>
> **potent**—*powerful; effective or efficacious*
> > a *potent* remedy
> > a *potent* idea
> > an Eastern *potentate* (ruler)
>
> **omnipotent**—*all-powerful*
> > *omnipotent* ruler
> > the old Greek *omnipotent* gods
>
> Also: **potential, possible, possess**

INCESSANT adj. *going on without interruption; unceasing; continuous*
En route to the vet's office, Meatloaf's *incessant* yowling drove us bats. Like many cats in a car, she cries continuously and pitifully—an *incessant* reminder that she never asked to go for a ride.

UNOBTRUSIVE adj. *not noticeable; inconspicuous; or, not aggressive*
Our pets Dude and Meatloaf don't know the word *unobtrusive*. Meatloaf thinks, why utter a dainty, *unobtrusive* mew when you can yowl? And Dude has spent his entire aggressive life seeking fights instead of being *unobtrusive*.

MEMORY FIX
To learn these new words, write each one on a sheet of paper. Also write a synonym or definition for each and say the words aloud as you work.

FILL IN THE BLANKS
Answers on page 243

> **To complete each sentence, select the correct noun form (as shown below) of the adjectives in List 4.**

fervor   indulgence   listlessness   profusion
uniformity superficiality vulnerability   unobtrusiveness

1 I object to the _____ of this assessment, especially since I had requested an in-depth evaluation.

2 By the end of our vacation, I had relaxed to the point of almost total _____!

3 We were excited by the _____ of the cheering crowd that lined the marathon runners' path.

4 In Glacier National Park in late June, the wildflowers erupt on the hills and roadsides in brilliant _____.

5 Realizing the _____ of animals on our planet, concerned people have organized to protect these dependent creatures.

6 "I'm begging your _____ for a minute," the speaker said, "while I digress briefly."

7 From a human's viewpoint, the owl that sleeps by day and hunts silently by night is a model of _____.

8 When we bake chocolate chip cookies, we try for _____ so that all of them have the same amount of chocolate.

TRUE OR FALSE   Answers on page 243

> Read each sentence below to see if the words in List 4 are being used properly. Then mark T (true) or F (false) beside each sentence.

1 If you've never really worked out at a health spa, the first experience is fun but a trifle *grueling*. _____

2 The painful twinges of out-of-shape muscles would be more acceptable if they were *incessant*. _____

3 His fondness for good company is only natural in a confirmed *recluse*. _____

4 Because his diving is still weak after years of practice, I think his *potential* is limited in that sport. _____

5 When a highway becomes treacherous, officials often *preclude* travel until conditions improve. _____

6 A pertinent anecdote is one that is *germane* to the topic. _____

7 The girl's *fervent* plea to the vet to save her beloved pet raccoon moved us to tears. _____

8 A planned, organized meeting cannot be termed *fortuitous.* _____

9 Erratic guidelines are more helpful than *uniform* ones. _____

10 An *unobtrusive* tooth fairy is the most successful. _____

MATCHING ANTONYMS Answers on page 233

> In column B, find two antonyms to explain each word in column A, and write their letters on the correct lines.

	A		B
_____	**1.** germane	**a.** irrelevant	**k.** restful
_____	**2.** profuse	**b.** weak	**l.** deeply serious
_____	**3.** uniform	**c.** aggressive	**m.** inappropriate
_____	**4.** grueling	**d.** restrained	**n.** stingy
_____	**5.** superficial	**e.** inconsistent	**o.** unforgiving
_____	**6.** potent	**f.** exhilarating	**p.** varied
_____	**7.** indulgent	**g.** thorough	**q.** ineffective
_____	**8.** listless	**h.** bouncy	**r.** friendly
_____	**9.** reclusive	**i.** gregarious	**s.** enthusiastic
_____	**10.** unobtrusive	**j.** critical	**t.** conspicuous

40

SNOOTS UP

---

arrogant • disdain • fastidious • haughty • disparage • deprecate • condescend • supercilious • contempt • pretentious • scoff • complacent

---

ARROGANT adj. *proud, overbearing; snootily self-important*
Despite his office, President Abraham Lincoln was never *arrogant*, but humble instead. A much later president, John F. Kennedy, said, "When power leads man toward *arrogance*, poetry reminds him of his limitations."

DISDAIN n. *scorn; snooty disapproval or dislike; contempt* v. **to disdain** adj. **disdainful**
No animal can show *disdain* as well as a cat. If Meatloaf's food is not quite right, she *disdains* to eat it and scratches around the bowl as if to bury the offending meal.

FASTIDIOUS adj. *extremely fussy and particular; meticulous*
A healthy cat is *fastidious* about its appearance and grooms its fur meticulously. A sick cat abandons this natural *fastidiousness*.

HAUGHTY adj. *openly and disdainfully proud; snooty* n. **hauteur, haughtiness**
You've heard that pride goes before a fall, but the old Biblical proverb actually says, "Pride goeth before destruction and a *haughty* spirit before a fall." You've seen *haughtiness*, that "I'm above you" attitude, right?

DISPARAGE v. *to belittle or downgrade (someone or something); to decry, depreciate, minimize*
When I was a kid, a bigger neighbor boy regularly *disparaged* my homemade tree house. I remember how that *disparagement* hurt and how it reduced my pride in my creation.

ROG = to ask

derogatory—*scornful, disparaging, downgrading, belittling*
>   of a *derogatory* nature
>   a highly *derogatory* critique

prerogative—*a special right or privilege*
>   a ruler's *prerogative*
>   her natural *prerogative* as the oldest

Also: **interrogate, arrogant, abrogate, surrogate**

DEPRECATE v. *to disapprove mildly, with regret*
adj. **deprecatory**, *hoping to avoid disapproval*
It's clear that Mom *deprecates* the mess in my room, but she understands that it's my space. When relatives are critical, Mom defends me with a *deprecatory* shrug and a smile.

CONDESCEND v. *to come down in level, unbend, stoop*
Meatloaf *condescends* to play hide-and-seek with Dude if she thinks no one will see her being kittenish again.

Likewise, my serious, formal grandfather will now and then *condescend* to listen to my rock music.

SUPERCILIOUS adj. *excessively proud; disdainfully superior*
Explaining her role in our school play, Amy said, "I'm playing an insufferably snooty lady, someone totally *supercilious*. I'm supposed to reek of *superciliousness* in every speech."

CONTEMPT n. *total lack of respect; disdain; scorn*
Our English class wrote essays on this Schopenhauer quote: "Hatred comes from the heart; *contempt* from the head; and neither feeling is quite within our control." That's probably true, but we can use *contempt* for good purposes, such as being openly *contemptuous* of those who damage our planet.

PRETENTIOUS adj. *showy, self-important, pompous; insisting on recognition, often unjustifiably*
The newly rich (nouveau riche, to my French teacher) often live in *pretentious* houses and drive expensive cars. *Pretentiousness* says, "Look at me. I'm important."

> **RID/RIS = to laugh**
>
> **deride**—*to mock or make fun of; to ridicule*
> > don't *deride* his shyness
> > humbled by his *derision*
>
> **risible**—*laughable, funny; used for laughter*
> > a truly *risible* situation
> > *risible* facial muscles
>
> Also: **ridicule, ridiculous, risibility, derisive, derisory**

SCOFF v. *to make fun of, mock; to belittle by jeering or contemptuous talk*
A few times we *scoffed* at guys who got pinned in the first period of their wrestling matches, but the coach stopped that. "Come out to support each other, not to *scoff*," he ordered.

COMPLACENT adj. *self-satisfied, smug*
Dude quivers all over with *complacency* after chasing off an intruder. As he returns to his position on our porch, he twitches his topknot *complacently*—smug in the knowledge that he's done his duty.

MEMORY FIX

To learn these new words, write each on a sheet of paper. Also, write a synonym or definition for each and say the words aloud as you work.

www.petersons.com

> **Choose the two words or phrases that best explain the meaning of each of the words in bold type.**

1 **fastidious**

(A) swift
(B) exceedingly particular
(C) meticulous
(D) unpleasant

2 **deprecate**

(A) reduce
(B) deny
(C) disapprove of
(D) regret

3 **arrogant**

(A) prideful
(B) questioning
(C) thoughtless
(D) overbearing

4 **condescend**

(A) stoop
(B) unbend
(C) forgive
(D) offend

5 **contempt**

(A) timely assistance
(B) scorn
(C) disdain
(D) refusal

6 **scoff**

(A) torture
(B) critique
(C) belittle
(D) mock or jeer

7 **complacent**

(A) smug
(B) self-satisfied
(C) peaceful
(D) well-located

8 prerogative

(A) annoyance
(B) privilege
(C) position
(D) right

9 deride

(A) scoff at
(B) dismount
(C) ridicule
(D) hoard

10 disparage

(A) resist
(B) minimize
(C) decry
(D) avoid

WORDS IN CONTEXT

Answers on page 244

> **Write the meaning of each *italicized* word on the lines provided.**

1 back stiffly erect, nose *haughtily* in the air

_____

2 filling an otherwise empty life with *pretentious* objects

_____

3 raised a *supercilious* eyebrow and gave a loud "Humph!"

_____

4 viewing the culprit with a look of utter *disdain*

_____

45

5 gentle cleric who *disdained* pulp literature

_____

6 cringing as he read the *derogatory* review

_____

7 insulted by their *condescending* manner

_____

8 enjoying my *prerogative* as the leader

_____

9 bowing her head in a *self-deprecatory* way

_____

10 regarding my handiwork with a certain

complacence

_____

ANALOGIES Answers on page 244

Choose the one word pair in each list below that expresses the same relationship as the pair in capital letters.

1 NAPOLEON : ARROGANCE

(A) Ben Franklin : hedonism
(B) Hitler : fastidiousness
(C) Tchaikovsky : bombast
(D) Twain : satire
(E) Maya Angelou : journalism

2 REMARK : DISPARAGING

(A) appearance : unobtrusive
(B) attitude : scoffing
(C) speech : articulate
(D) article : meticulous
(E) design : risible

3 PRIDE : HAUTEUR

    (A) pretentiousness : wealth
    (B) disdain : disgust
    (C) sorrow : contempt
    (D) satisfaction : complacency
    (E) youth : vulnerability

4 DERISION : RIDICULE

    (A) sweetness : indulgence
    (B) disdain : honor
    (C) prerogative : duty
    (D) seclusion : profusion
    (E) scorn : contempt

REVIEW: LISTS 1–5

Here's one more chance to practice using the words in lists 1–5. But first, read each list and say each word and its meaning out loud. More than one third of us learn best through our EARS.

FIND THE ODDBALL Answers on page 234

> In each word group, cross out the oddball—the one unrelated word or phrase.

1 bigot phony hypocrite heretic fake

2 ridicule derision hauteur disdain derogation

3 insist assent comply yield acquiesce

4 clamorous noisy vociferous persistently vocal nasty

5 articulate hyperbole lucid effective clear

6 relevant pertinent germane interesting related to

7 provoke preclude forestall hinder prevent

8 proud inevitable arrogant haughty supercilious

9 flatterer toady sycophant brownnoser hedonist

10 hackneyed terse clipped concise succinct

TRUE OR FALSE

Answers on page 244

> **Check these sentences for correctness. Then mark T (true) or F (false) beside each.**

1 *Euphemisms* allow you to say in public what would otherwise be unacceptable or possibly even cruel. _____

2 *Hackneyed* phrases, such as "he eats like a horse" or "she's thin as a rail," are not examples of *hyperbole*. _____

3 You should avoid hiring speakers who are very *eloquent*. _____

4 You shouldn't *verify* data for a research paper. _____

5 *Hedonists* are careful to avoid parties. _____

6 A *miser* enjoys supporting several charities. _____

7 *Zealots*, or *fanatics*, rarely *condone* ideologies that run counter to theirs and may even *disparage* contrasting views in a most *articulate* manner. _____

8 In *My Family and Other Animals*, Gerald Durrell pokes fun at everyone in his family, thereby creating a book-length *lampoon*. _____

9 As an ancient Greek general, you might wish to consult the famous *oracle* at Delphi before a battle. _____

49

10 If you prefer short meetings, select *loquacious* board members, not *laconic* ones. _____

FIND THE SYNONYM Answers on page 244

> From the choices offered, select the missing synonym for each numbered word group and write that synonym on the corresponding line.

to concur	to condone	charlatan	profuse
precursor	banal	inexorable	listless
to chastise	equivocal	grueling	potent

1 unclear   evasive   confusing   undecided _____

2 to agree   coincide   assent   approve _____

3 trite   hackneyed   commonplace   stale _____

4 languid   indifferent   uncaring _____

5 to scold   castigate   punish   censure _____

6 impostor   quack   fraud   cheat _____

7 to overlook   excuse   pardon _____

8 forerunner   harbinger   herald _____

9 immovable   relentless   inflexible _____

10 punishing   tiring   demanding   exhausting _____

11 abundant   bountiful   lavish   lush _____

12 powerful   effective   efficacious _____

50

WHO SAID THAT?

Answers on page 234

From the choices offered, write the *type of speaker* for each of the following comments.

raconteur	glutton	skeptic	interrogator
equivocator	heretic	recluse	orator
despot	insurgent	scoffer	deprecator

1 "Friends, Romans, countrymen, lend me your ears."_____

2 Did I tell you the one about Anansi the Spider and his cousin . . .? _____

3 Could I have another steak? _____

4 It's peaceful here alone on the island. _____

5 Are you sure? Did you run tests that prove your ideas are actual facts? _____

6 Clean your room now or else! _____

7 Gee, there's nothing like a good uprising. _____

8 That's nothing. I was riding a bike at age three. _____

9 I don't believe that anymore; I can't. _____

10 Well, maybe and maybe not. It sort of seems that way, and then again it doesn't. _____

11 I repeat. Is that your toad in the soup? _____

12 I didn't really mean to, she said, shrugging. _____

51

MATCHING

Answers on page 234

> **Match the words in column A with their meanings in column B and then write the meanings in the space provided.**

A	B
_____ 1. coalesce	pompous language
_____ 2. laud	accidental
_____ 3. cursory	to ridicule
_____ 4. bombast	disdain, scorn
_____ 5. platitude	to scatter or fan out
_____ 6. aver	to obliterate; wear away
_____ 7. fortuitous	lenient
_____ 8. deride	continuous

_____ 9. prerogative	to praise
_____ 10. contempt	superficial or hasty
_____ 11. augment	to come together
_____ 12. disperse	to declare firmly
_____ 13. efface	banality
_____ 14. indulgent	to increase
_____ 15. incessant	right or privilege

52

6 VERBS TO HEED

garner • mar • heed • meander • nullify • obliterate • mitigate • obscure • peruse • raze • placate • rebuff

GARNER v. *to gather or collect; accumulate; earn*
Our paper's sports editor *garners* all the information he can about an opponent before a crucial game. He says, "I go to their practices with the goal of *garnering* any clue, however small, that will help us to compete better."

MAR v. *to spoil or damage; to injure or blemish*
We all hate having something nice *marred*. For instance, a zit really *mars* a person's appearance. When flying gravel *marred* the paint on Dad's new car, he went ballistic.

HEED v. *to listen to, pay attention to, consider; to mind*
Meatloaf *heeds* our orders only if she feels like it. Deep in a cat's soul must be the motto: To *Heed* is To Yield Independence. One day, *heedless* of our pleading, Meatloaf made her way to the top of the neighbor's giant oak.

MEANDER v. *to wander casually with no set plan; to ramble*
A speech should not *meander* but should follow a clear outline; nor should an airplane *meander* through the skies. But I'm glad that streams and creeks *meander* in no set pattern across the countryside.

NULLIFY v. *to render unimportant or without worth; to negate or invalidate; to annul legally*
The Student Council voted to *nullify* some regulations passed by former councils. We made them "*null* and void," as the expression goes.

OBLITERATE v. *to erase completely, wiping out all traces*

MUT/MUTAT = to change

immutable—*changeless and unchanging; unalterable, eternal*

> Nature's *immutable* laws
> the *immutable* power of love

mutation—*significant genetic change; the one changed*

> a *mutation* in the human form that evolved over time scientifically engineered *mutations* in corn plants

Also: **mutable, mutant, commute, permutation, transmutation**

A group of us watched from a high dune as the tide came in and *obliterated* our sand castles, leaving the shore flat and smooth. I wish I could *obliterate* those old, childish nightmares.

MITIGATE v. *to ease, making less severe; to alleviate or relieve*

We slathered antihistamine cream on Amy's bee stings, hoping to *mitigate* the pain. She said that the burning and itching were somewhat *mitigated* but certainly not obliterated.

OBSCURE v. *to make dim or unclear; to conceal, hide* adj. **obscure**, *vague, mysterious, remote, dark*

As a wrestler, I like to *obscure* the real objective of my movements and catch an opponent off guard. Chess and checkers players *obscure* their strategies, too, I'm sure.

PON/POS = to place or put

posit—*to suppose, propose, suggest; to assume or affirm*

> let's *posit* this theory
> when he first *posited* that idea

proponent—*one who talks in favor of something, an advocate*

> a famous *proponent* of exercise
> hardly a *proponent* of sloth

Also: **position, postpone, component, exponent, repository, expose, depose, transpose, deposit, dispose, juxtapose**

54

PERUSE v. *to study or examine carefully* n. **perusal**
The guidance counselors urged us to *peruse* the booklet *Taking the SAT*. Also, they suggested we *peruse* a self-help book that explains each kind of problem. After a *perusal* of *The Ultimate SAT Toolkit*, I decided I needed to brush up on geometry.

RAZE v. *to tear down completely, to demolish*
We spent last weekend *razing* the old barn on our property. We'd hoped to save it, but since it was too decrepit to restore, we were forced to *raze* it instead.

PLACATE v. *to calm, soothe, or appease, especially by offering to "be nice" or to do someone a favor*
Last year's seniors were a crazy bunch, always in trouble and trying to *placate* the principal for what they'd done. As time went by, she said she couldn't be *placated* any longer.

REBUFF v. *to criticize harshly or to reject someone, often by snubbing them (ignoring them)*
Meatloaf *rebuffed* Dude's offers of puppy friendship when he first joined our family. Do you think a dog feels hurt the way a human does when he suffers a *rebuff*? Dude didn't allow himself to be *rebuffed* for long, of course.

MEMORY FIX
To learn these new words, write each one on a sheet of paper. Also write a synonym or definition for each and say the words aloud as you work.

RHYME TIME Answers on page 245

> **Complete these couplets of pretty awful poetry with the correct form of one of the new words in List 6.**

1 An unusual word that at first makes us frown,

To _____ a building means to tear it down!

2 Something _____ forever stays the same,

Unlike that fleeting idol called fame.

3 The detective announced, "A theory I'll

_____ .

The criminal's hiding right here in this closet."

4 Down fragrant paths of rose and oleander,

My love and I were happy to _____ .

(Oh, brother.)

5 A _____ is a really odd star for a show,

But remember those Ninja turtles we know?

MATCHING Answers on page 245

> **Choose the two words or phrases that best explain the meaning of each of the words in bold type.**

1 **mar**
- (A) blemish
- (B) confuse
- (C) spoil
- (D) annoy

2 **mitigate**
- (A) discuss
- (B) adjust
- (C) relieve
- (D) alleviate

3 obliterate

(A) disguise
(B) efface
(C) wipe out
(D) cover up

4 rebuff

(A) snub
(B) restore
(C) polish
(D) reject

5 garner

(A) avoid
(B) collect
(C) strew around
(D) accumulate

6 obscure

(A) cloud over
(B) conceal
(C) caution
(D) negate

7 peruse

(A) scan
(B) memorize
(C) study carefully
(D) examine

8 meander

(A) walk
(B) wander
(C) ramble
(D) flirt

9 placate

(A) enjoy
(B) entertain
(C) soothe
(D) appease

10 raze

(A) lift up
(B) tear down
(C) devour
(D) demolish

11 nullify

   (A) invalidate
   (B) join legally
   (C) end
   (D) negate

12 heed

   (A) wait on
   (B) mind or obey
   (C) consider
   (D) learn

SUBSTITUTION   Answers on page 245

> **Replace each italicized word or phrase with the correct word from the word list in this unit, including words from roots.**

1 I refuse to *pay attention to* that wacko advice!

   _____

2 She's always been a *person in favor* of recycling.

   _____

3 That splash of aftershave certainly *spoiled* the tabletop. _____

4 The digressive nature of his lecture unfortunately *made dim, mysterious, and unclear* his major points. _____

5 Her explanation should *soothe and relieve* Claire's anger. _____

6 Queen Elizabeth I *firmly rejected* those who even hinted that the English Navy might lose to the Spanish Armada. _____

7 We were finally able to *make promises of never doing that again,* Mom and Dad, but it wasn't easy. _____

8 I spent hours *studying carefully* the driver's manual before I took the test. _____

9 As long as they adhere to the Constitution, members of the Supreme Court may *render null and void* a decision by a lower court. _____

10 At summer meets with neighboring towns, Amy has *collected* several awards for backstroke and freestyle swimming. _____

BEWARE A PARSIMONIOUS PREDECESSOR

virtuoso • termerity • volition • torpor • quandary • trepidation • zenith • reticence • respite • parsimony • nostalgia • predecessor

VIRTUOSO n. *a highly skilled performer*
As Meatloaf yowled eloquently from the top of the oak tree, Dad observed, "Hmm, we have a true feline *virtuoso*. Now if only she were a *virtuoso* at climbing, she could get herself down from there."

TEMERITY n. *unwise boldness; rash or reckless behavior*
Meatloaf showed unusual *temerity* in scaling that oak. Dude, of course, is forever hurtling into danger with a *temerity* that would never occur to a more sensible dog.

VOLITION n. *use of your own will, by your choice*
Animals were once viewed as beings of instinct only, with no powers of *volition*. Now we know that animals act on their own *volition* fairly often.

TORPOR n. *sluggishness, lethargy; inability to think or act quickly* adj. **torpid**
To be absolutely pooped is to feel *torpor*. I was in a totally *torpid* state once after a grueling wrestling match. Boxers must feel a similar *torpor* after their matches.

QUANDARY n. *a feeling of puzzlement or doubt*
Choosing a college is a perplexing process that has most of us in a state of *quandary*. It's a *quandary* that will remain, I think, until the final decision is made.

TREPIDATION n. *fear, worry, apprehension*
I keep seeing the phrase "in fear and *trepidation*," which seems repetitious, because *trepidation* often

---
ARCH = chief or main; ruler

hierarchy—*a series arranged by rank or grade*
> at the top of the *hierarchy*
> her place in the *hierarchy*

anarchy—*lack of government, often resulting in lawlessness*
> historical *anarchy* in the Balkans
> *anarchy* in the ranks

Also: **patriarch, matriarch, monarch, archangel, architect**

---

means fear. I'd rather say, "He went forward timidly, with *trepidation*."

ZENITH n. *the highest point or acme; point of culmination*
Although *zenith* means the highest point in the sky above us, I more often hear it used in phrases like "when his powers were at their *zenith*" or "at the *zenith* of her career."

RETICENCE n. *quietness and restraint in personality* adj. **reticent**, *silent, restrained, reserved*

President Calvin Coolidge, a silent, restrained New Englander, was famous for his *reticence*. On hearing that this most *reticent* of men had died, writer Dorothy Parker said, "How can you tell?"

RESPITE n. *time of relief from activity; rest, pause, lull*
Thanksgiving weekend came as a welcome *respite* after a crazy autumn. That's the purpose of a vacation, of course—to act as a *respite* from our normal, busy lives.

PARSIMONY n. *extreme stinginess; thrift; penny-pinching*
As all of Dickens's readers know, the character Ebenezer Scrooge is synonymous with *parsimony*. Underpaying his staff and failing to heat his business office were only a few of Scrooge's *parsimonious* habits.

NOSTALGIA n. *a sentimental longing for a past time or state* adj. **nostalgic**
My grandparents are a typically *nostalgic* pair who always tell the same stories about my dad as a kid.

Nostalgia for the past and the way things were must be a natural part of growing older.

LU/LUC = light

lucid—*clear and distinct; sensible, intelligible*
  a graceful, *lucid* talk
  having recovered *lucid* speech

elucidate—*to explain fully and clearly*
  elucidate his problem, please
  always happy to *elucidate*

Also: **lucidity, translucent, luminous, Lucifer, lucubration**

PREDECESSOR n. *an ancestor; prior person in a position*
My *predecessor* on the newspaper was an editor who turned the various staff members into a close family of coworkers. My grandparents, who are my hereditary *predecessors* and who aren't one bit parsimonious, generously provide a vacation spot for our entire family each summer.

MEMORY FIX
To learn these new words, write each one on a sheet of paper. Also write a synonym or definition for each and say the words aloud as you work.

FILL IN THE BLANKS
Answers on page 245

From the new words in List 7, select the one that best completes the meaning and logic of each sentence. Note which tense or form of the word is required for sense.

1 Meadowlark Lemon, a magician on the basketball court, and Itzhak Perlman, a gifted violinist, are both _____ in their respective fields.

2 The alternatives were so different and so complex that I was left in a complete _____ .

3 When the anaesthetic has worn off and the patient is _____ , the newspaper reporter will interview him.

4 A _____ man, Jacob Grunch amassed a fortune through careful management and total disregard of others' needs.

5 I wouldn't mind crossing the desert at night, but never when the sun is at its _____ !

6 _____ in every limb of his body, the hibernating bear stretched slowly, then settled back into sleep.

7 I remember my summers at camp with _____ , sorry that I'm too old to return.

8 Before the principal called him to her office, my friend Greg went of his own _____ , hoping to mitigate her anger by his voluntary appearance.

9 Today's politicians don't dare be _____ folk, because the TV era demands articulate speakers.

10 We're amazed every year at the _____ of the squirrels who collect acorns from our porch, despite the vigilance of Meatloaf and Dude.

MATCHING ANTONYMS Answers on page 235

> **Knowing opposites is helpful. Match the words on the left with their opposites on the right.**

_____	**1.** trepidation*	to obscure
_____	**2.** reticence	descendant
_____	**3.** zenith	hyperactive
_____	**4.** torpid	order
_____	**5.** temerity	confidence
_____	**6.** elucidate	beginner
_____	**7.** anarchy	generosity
_____	**8.** virtuoso	nadir (lowest point)
_____	**9.** predecessor	bombast
_____	**10.** parsimony	timidity

* Knowing what trepidation is, what does *intrepid* probably mean? _____

FIND THE ODDBALL

Answers on page 235

> **In each word group below, cross out the oddball—the one unrelated word or phrase.**

1 ranking hierarchy assortment series

2 break angle rest lull respite

3 niece ancestor grandparent predecessor

4 instinct will volition desire

5 apprehension worry temperament trepidation

6 quest preplexity quandary puzzlement

7 betrayal stinginess miserliness parsimony

8 transparent coherent intelligible lucid

9 rashness fear boldness temerity

10 quaintness restraint silence reticence

THAT'S ME!

---

astute • discerning • formidable • indefatigable • sage • profound • judicious • meticulous • painstaking • resilient • tenacious • benevolent

---

ASTUTE adj. *wise, shrewd, perceptive; perspicacious*
Like everyone in my class, I hope to make a fairly *astute* college selection. Luckily, our guidance counselors are pros and have made several *astute* suggestions that will help me to narrow my choices.

DISCERNING adj. *showing wisdom and wise judgment; discriminating wisely among choices* v. **to discern** n. **discernment**
Emily Dickinson wrote, "Much Madness is divinest Sense—To a *discerning* eye." My class wrote short essays on that couplet, trying to *discern* its meaning.

We're gradually becoming *discerning* readers and interpreters of poetry.

FORMIDABLE adj. *fostering respect or awe; arousing fear; redoubtable*
Because the opponents I'd normally face in our next wrestling meet are *formidable* beyond belief, I have to sweat down to the next lowest weight class in order to wrestle competitively. Of course, nothing helps a guy sweat like the fear of a *formidable* adversary!

INDEFATIGABLE adj. *untiring, tireless (see root of "fatigue")*
Mom's *indefatigable* determination to learn computer programming is amazing. Our whole family is stubborn, though, so the word *indefatigable* often applies to us.

SAGE adj. *wise as a result of experience and thought; shrewd and discerning of judgment; prudent* adj. **sagacious**, *shrewd* n. **sage**, *wise elder*
Look at all the meaning *sage* conveys in only four letters. Perhaps author Ernest Hemingway made a very *sage* decision by using mostly short, punchy words.

PROFOUND adj. *intellectually deep; deeply important; complete or all-encompassing*

Our new principal is a *profoundly* thoughtful man, given to uttering *profound* thoughts whenever they occur to him. This talkativeness is a *profound* change from his predecessor, who was extremely reticent.

JUDICIOUS adj. *showing good judgment; wise, discreet*

I always think of *judge*, *justice*, and *jury* when I see the root *ju*, an old root of Jove and Zeus that actually means "shining sky." Of course, gods have always been thought to live in the sky and to be the most *judicious* of beings.

METICULOUS adj. *particular down to the tiniest detail*

Meatloaf is a *meticulous* groomer. This care results in a glossy fur coat that advertises her *meticulous* nature.

PAINSTAKING adj. *revealing much care and effort*

With *painstaking* care, I restored the used car that I inherited on my eighteenth birthday. In the true sense of the word *painstaking*, I took great pains to wash, paint, and wax every inch of this incredible treasure.

RESILIENT adj. *elastic; able to "snap back" after change or misfortune* n. **resilience**
Dude's personality is *resilient*; he bounces back to his cheerful, optimistic self within minutes of being scolded. Without this natural *resilience*, he'd be sorrowful much of the time, because he gets frequently corrected.

TENACIOUS adj. *persistent in holding on (as "barnacles are tenacious"); retentive (as "a tenacious mind")* n. **tenacity,** *courage*
If I had a more *tenacious* mind, I'd be able to remember history dates and math formulas better.

Luckily, I'm a pretty *tenacious* wrestler—a real bulldog.

BENEVOLENT adj. *showing good will (Also from bene = good "benefactor," "benign," "beneficent," etc.)*
In world history we studied Charlemagne, an educated and *benevolent* French king who ruled for the good of his people. We debated the virtues of a *benevolent* dictatorship in class.

MEMORY FIX
To learn these new words, write each on a sheet of paper. Also write a synonym or definition for each and say the words aloud as you work.

FIND THE SYNONYM Answers on page 245

> From the choices offered below, select the
> missing synonym for each word group and write
> it in the space provided.

astute   resilient   tenacious   alleviate   tenet
profound   formidable   meticulous   untenable

1 awesome inspiring fear redoubtable _____

2 deeply intellectual all-encompassing _____

3 indefensible   unable to be inhabited _____

4 belief dogma principle doctrine _____

5 able to spring back to form   elastic _____

6 perceptive shrewd wise perspicacious
_____

7 extremely careful   attentive to detail _____

8 persistent   determined   retentive _____

9 relieve   lessen   lighten   reduce _____

TRUE OR FALSE Answers on page 245

> Read each sentence to see if it makes sense. Then
> mark T (true) or F (false) beside each.

1 Every bit of homework requires *indefatigable*
effort. _____

2 By definition, a *benefactor* is usually *benevolent*.
_____

3 Being *meticulous* about your appearance for a job
interview is probably a waste of time. _____

69

4 If you insert the end of a stout board beneath that boulder, you'll have the *leverage* needed to move the rock. _____

5 The cult leader's insistence that he was Jesus Christ put him in an *untenable* position.

_____

6 No one bothers to try to *alleviate* the symptoms of poison ivy. _____

7 Typically, *painstaking* folks are among the most prized in hospital operating rooms. _____

8 Rarely can you arrive at a *judicious* decision in seconds. _____

9 If you have to have a tumor, let's hope it's *benign*. _____

10 *Discerning* which chocolate chip cookies should win the blue ribbon would be a disgusting job.

_____

11 The last quality you'd want in a fight is *tenacity*.

_____

ANALOGIES Answers on page 235

Choose the one word pair in each list below that expresses the same relationship as the pair in capital letters.

1 LAWYER : ASTUTE

(A) artist : insightful
(B) chemist : beneficent
(C) pathologist : painstaking
(D) instructor : resilient
(E) detective : awe-inspiring

2 PROFOUND : THOUGHTFUL

(A) meticulous : painstaking
(B) judicious : discreet
(C) shrewd : astute
(D) sagacious : bright
(E) fearful : terrified

3 SUPREME COURT : SAGACITY

(A) swimmer : tenacity
(B) bones : tension
(C) symphony : benevolence
(D) muscles : resilience
(E) city council : tenure

4 FORMIDABLE : DEFENSE

(A) indefatigable : enemy
(B) perspicacious : tenant
(C) judicious : friend
(D) discernible : traitor
(E) redoubtable : warrior

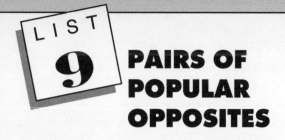

PAIRS OF POPULAR OPPOSITES

abstract/concrete • lax/stringent • atrophy/burgeon • affluent/indigent • cacophony/euphony • optimism/pessimism • gravity/levity • desecrate/consecrate • resolute/irresolute • objective/subjective • refutable/irrefutable

ABSTRACT adj. *indefinite; vague; theoretical; intangible*
CONCRETE adj. *definite or specific; real, tangible*
When I watch our team captain wrestle, I'm seeing a *concrete* display of courage, which is itself an *abstract* concept. Friendship is another *abstraction*, but my friends are real, *concrete* human beings.

LAX adj. *loose; unstructured; not firm; negligent; slack*
STRINGENT adj. *tight or constricted; rigid, adhering firmly to accepted standards*
At orientation for new counselors, the camp director handed us a *stringent* set of rules for the camp. "If rules are dangerously *lax*," he said, "we have a dangerous camp."

ATROPHY v. *to wither, degenerate; to waste away*
BURGEON v. *to flourish; to grow and quickly expand; bloom*
Ideas *burgeon* in people's minds just as flowers or weeds *burgeon* in soil. By contrast, anything that *atrophies* is faring poorly, like muscles that *atrophy* from illness.

AFFLUENT adj. *wealthy in a material sense*
INDIGENT adj. *very poor; lacking necessary material goods*
A guest lecturer at our school spoke on the contrast between Haiti's few *affluent* people and all the

72

PHON = sound

phonics—*a system of sounds for letters, groups of letters, and syllables; acoustics, the science of sound*
> learned *phonics* early in school
> a new *phonics* system

symphony—*harmonious musical composition; symphony orchestra*
> beauty of a Beethoven *symphony*
> the Boston *Symphony*

Also: **telephone, sousaphone, phonetics, phonograph, euphony, cacophony**

---

others—people so *indigent* that they live on the hills in three-sided shacks.

CACOPHONY n. *displeasing, harsh sound; horrible noise*
EUPHONY n. *pleasing or sweet sound; harmony (of speech)*
Parents and kids have different ideas about *euphonious* sound. Our folks often call our music *cacophony* when it is absolute *euphony* to us. Any judgment about *cacophony* versus *euphony* seems pretty subjective.

OPTIMISM n. *a positive, upbeat, favorable outlook on life*
PESSIMISM n. *a negative, discouraging outlook on life*
For Mark Twain, Tom Sawyer represented *optimism*. Huck Finn, who was a stark realist, embodied *pessimism*. Comics joke that a *pessimist* is a person who has all the facts. An *optimist*, of course, focuses on the encouraging facts.

GRAVITY n. *weighty importance; seriousness*
LEVITY n. *lightness of approach or treatment; humor*
We probably should treat the SATs with *gravity*, as the results can make a big difference in our lives. But I'm not just a number, and my score doesn't say who I am. My friends and I joke about SATs a lot, because *levity* helps us get past tough challenges.

DESECRATE v. *to defile or profane something sacred or very special*

www.petersons.com

CONSECRATE v. *to make sacred or holy or worthy of respect; to hallow*

Most Americans don't want anyone to *desecrate* our flag, our national anthem, or our monuments—anything that has special, emotional significance to us. Those things have been *consecrated* over time in our culture.

RESOLUTE adj. *firmly determined; steady; faithful*
IRRESOLUTE adj. *uncertain about behavior; vacillating*

I acted in a totally *resolute* manner last Halloween when I took some neighbor kids through a famous "haunted house." If I'd seemed nervous or *irresolute* for even a second, those kids would have bolted like spooked horses.

OBJECTIVE adj. *lacking personal feeling or involvement; in a detached, unbiased, fair manner*
SUBJECTIVE adj. *colored by personal feeling or opinion*

All kids wish that the grading of writing were more *objective* than it is; unfortunately, *subjective* factors always creep in. Our English teachers mark one grade on papers for the *objective* items like grammar, with a separate grade for creativity, which is a more *subjective* judgment.

REFUTABLE adj. *shaky in foundation, therefore able to be refuted (proved wrong or false)*
IRREFUTABLE adj. *impossible to refute (prove wrong or false)*

My lawyer cousin said he's only interested in *irrefutable* evidence that can't be disproved in court. *Refutable* evidence is clearly worthless.

MEMORY FIX

To learn these new words, write each one on a sheet of paper. Also write a synonym or definition for each and say the words aloud as you work.

WORD ANALYSIS Answers on page 246

> **Fill in the blanks in the sentences below based on the word list in List 9.**

1 Euphonious sound makes you feel _____, contrasted with cacophony, which is _____.

2 The _____ sees the glass as half full; the _____ sees it as half empty.

3 Psychologists say that somewhat _____, dependable rules provide children the necessary "fences" needed for security, whereas _____, unstable guidelines undermine their security.

4 _____ judgments are unclouded by emotion, whereas _____ judgments reflect the feelings of the judge.

5 A poem is a _____ thing; poetry itself, an idea.

6 We speak of plants as things that _____ and grow, then eventually wither. Ideas or muscles that waste away or wither are said to _____ from lack of use.

7 The _____ 1980s saw people busily acquiring luxuries, not just the necessities of life, which _____ people lack.

8 Humor provides the _____ that enables us to survive the _____ of situations beyond our control.

9 We _____ the senior medallion in the entryway of our school with a solemn ceremony. Any underclassman who _____ it will be dead meat.

10 Mom's _____ skill with homemade brownies was proved at the last bake sale. Now, if she says we don't need her brownies at a bake sale, that notion will be easily _____ .

11 The Cowardly Lion was a timid, _____ fellow in the Oz books, but as soon as he had courage he behaved in a most _____ manner, full of determination.

USING THE WORDS   Answers on page 246

> **Write the new words from List 9 on the correct lines below.**

1 to wither away = _____

to flourish, bloom = _____

2 can't be proved wrong = _____

apt to be disproved = _____

3 impersonal = _____

   colored by feeling = _____

4 to profane = _____

   to hallow = _____

5 vague, indefinite = _____

   definite, real = _____

6 loose, lenient = _____

   tight, rigid = _____

7 horrible noise = _____

   pleasing sound = _____

8 rosy outlook = _____

   negative outlook = _____

9 seriousness = _____

   lightness, humor = _____

10 firmly determined = _____

   unsure, vacillating = _____

LIST 10 THE BLUES

irascible • writhe • taciturn • tawdry •
servile • surreptitious • rancor • sullen •
remorse • rue • malice • malign

IRASCIBLE adj. *easily angered; testy, choleric, touchy*
Irascible after her bath at the vet's, Meatloaf snarled at Dude and me and then hid under the sofa. Poor Meatloaf. She's usually a pussycat, not an *irascible* grouch.

WRITHE v. *to twist; twist sideways in pain or suffering*
Writhing from side to side is the natural movement of snakes like the Southwestern sidewinder. When people *writhe*, they are either suffering pain or perhaps danc-ing. I've done a bit of *writhing* myself, on the wrestling mat.

TACITURN adj. *naturally silent, untalkative; laconic*
A *taciturn* person would enjoy this George Eliot quote: "Blessed be the person who has nothing to say and who refrains from giving wordy evidence to that fact."

TAWDRY adj. *cheap-looking; showy, gaudy* n. **tawdry,** *showy, cheap finery*
Tawdry is a bit of British history that became a word. St. Audrey's laces were wispy silk necklaces sold for the saint's feast day. The words St. Audrey were run together, and '*taudrey's* laces were actually cheap and showy, so a new word gradually evolved.

SERVILE adj. *subservient, abject, annoyingly submissive*
Amy's latest role cast her as a *servile* maid who is always whining, "Anythin' more, yer lordship?" I dislike that *servile*, cringing attitude because it seems hypocritical.

MON/MONIT = warn, advise, remind

admonish—*to warn strongly, reprove; show disapproval*

> she *admonished* the kittens not to lose their mittens

premonition—*forewarning or foreboding; presentiment*

> a *premonition* of disaster
> troubled by *premonitions*

Also: **admonition, monitor, remonstrate, monument**

SURREPTITIOUS adj. *secretive, deceptive; clandestine*

Does everybody take *surreptitious* little bites of cookie dough? Or *surreptitious* peeks at letters not addressed to them?

RANCOR n. *deep-seated bitterness; old enmity*

I've seen this cliché several times: "He viewed his old foe with *rancor*," and I know from experience that *rancor* is a bitter feeling.

SULLEN adj. *quietly resentful; lowering; gloomy, dismal*

For an understanding of the word *sullen*, it's hard to beat Robert Burns's lines in *Tam o'Shanter*: "Whare sits our sulky, *sullen* dame, Gathering her brows like gathering storm, Nursing her wrath to keep it warm."

REMORSE adj. *self-reproach, regret; a guilty uneasiness*

I feel some *remorse* if I squash a ladybug, because they're harmless, but I never regret flattening a wasp or bumblebee. I doubt that a wasp feels *remorse* when it stings me.

RUE v. *to regret exceedingly; feel remorse or sorrow*

Gramma is always saying I'll "*rue* the day" I became a car owner, and the poet A. E. Housman warned that giving your heart to a girl results in "endless *rue*." If I believe them, I'll be regretting something all my life!

MALICE n. *the desire to see another suffer; extreme ill will or spite* adj. **malicious**

A disillusioned Mark Twain wrote in his *Autobiography*: "Of the entire brood, he [man] is the only one—the solitary one—that possesses *malice*.

That is the basest of all instincts, passions, vices—the most hateful . . . He is the only creature that inflicts pain for sport, knowing it to *be* pain. . . ."

MALIGN n. *to slander, defame; speak of in an ill-willed manner*

Although we've published critical profiles in the school paper, we've never actually *maligned* anyone's character. Tabloids thrive on *maligning* famous people, but our staff regards that as yellow journalism.

MEDI = middle

mediate—*to reconcile by acting as an intermediary or go-between in a dispute*
> happy to *mediate* for both sides
> involved in *mediation*

mediocre—*of only ordinary quality or low quality*
> unfortunately *mediocre* performance
> only *mediocre* at best

Also: **mediator, intermediate, medium, medieval**

MEMORY FIX

To learn these new words, write each one on a sheet of paper. Also write a synonym or definition for each and say the words aloud as you work.

FILL IN THE BLANKS   Answers on page 246

> Using the new words and roots in List 10, select the one that best fits the meaning and logic of each phrase.

1 an _____ , demanding boss who quickly lost her temper

2 still brooded on it years later, consumed by _____

3 an uneasy _____ that something would go wrong

4 reading the book _____ under the covers at night

5 reduced a touching story to a cheap, _____ thriller

6 gave us a cheerful, forgiving look, not a _____ one

7 _____ on the sidewalk in pain after spraining an ankle

8 working at replacing with charity the _____ he once felt

9 a naturally withdrawn, _____ personality who feels little need for talk

10 wearing the typical _____ look of a sycophant or toady

11 spoken with cruelty and _____ , meant to be hurtful

12 to feel strong regret or remorse is to _____ something

For each word in column A, find two
synonymous words or phrases in column B and
write their letters on the appropriate lines at the
left.

	A		**B**	
_____	**1.** remorse	**a.** slander	**k.** forewarning	
_____		**b.** laconic	**l.** quietly resentful	
_____	**2.** premonition	**c.** bitterness	**m.** guilty unease	
_____		**d.** cheap	**n.** defame	
_____	**3.** malign	**e.** secretive	**o.** deceptive	
_____		**f.** foreboding	**p.** lowering	
_____	**4.** sullen	**g.** subservient	**q.** silent	
_____		**h.** self-reproach	**r.** choleric	

_____	**5.** rancor	**i.** testy	**s.** gaudy
_____		**j.** abject	**t.** old enmity
_____	**6.** tawdry		
_____			
_____	**7.** surreptitious		
_____			
_____	**8.** taciturn		
_____			
_____	**9.** servile		
_____			
_____	**10.** irascible		

82

RHYME TIME

Answers on page 246

Complete these couplets of pretty awful poetry* with the correct form of one of the new words in List 10.

1 It's me and Jane Fonda, lean and lithe,

But some days this twist is a painful _____ .

2 Regretful, sorrowful, sorry Sue,

Hers is a heart laden with _____ .

3 Children are _____ in Mother Goose rhyme,

To be careful, watch out, and be home on time.

_____

* Okay, *terrible* poetry.

4 Nasty and mean was witchy old Alice,

Her mind just brimmed with spite and

_____ .

5 Folks whose mental skills are _____

Should perhaps think twice before playing poker.

6 To _____ is to resolve a dispute,

By compromise, not by acting cute.

83

REVIEW: LISTS 6–10

Reviewing is the best way to keep these words forever. First, reread lists 6–10, saying each word aloud. You, too, may be someone who learns best through your ears.

FIND THE SYNONYM   Answers on page 236

From the choices offered below, find the missing synonym for each word group and write it in the space provided.

obscure	immutable	mitigate	burgeon
lucid	respite	abstract	taciturn
astute	parsimonious	sacrilege	resolute

1 dark   vague   mysterious   remote _____

2 alleviate   ease   relieve   lessen _____

3 unchanging   eternal   unalterable _____

4 break   rest   pause   lull _____

5 stingy   penny-pinching   miserly _____

6 distinct   clear   sensible   intelligible _____

7 perspicacious   shrewd   wise   perceptive _____

8 indefinite   theoretical   intangible _____

9 flourish   grow   blossom   bloom _____

10 determined   faithful   steady _____

11 desecration   fouling   profaning _____

84

12 laconic   silent   untalkative   reticent

_____

ANALOGIES Answers on page 247

> Choose the one word pair in each list below that expresses the same relationship as the pair in capital letters.

1 SYMPHONY : VIOLINS

(A) admonition : manager
(B) council : agenda
(C) choir : music
(D) religion : tenets
(E) jury : oaths

2 ENERGY : TORPOR

(A) holiness : consecration
(B) government : anarchy
(C) phonics : speech
(D) thought : discernment
(E) heaviness : gravity

3 SIN : REMORSEFUL

(A) shack : tawdry
(B) mistake : rueful
(C) carelessness : marred
(D) problem : refuted
(E) error : hopeful

4 PAST : NOSTALGIA

(A) time : abstraction
(B) sun : zenith
(C) present : pessimism
(D) philosophy : perusal
(E) future : optimism

5 MEDIATE : SAGE

(A) placate : sister
(B) meander : guide
(C) elucidate : teacher
(D) posit : parent
(E) refute : director

6 BATTLE : TREPIDATION

    (A)   acquaintance : levity
    (B)   general : hierarchy
    (C)   enemy : rancor
    (D)   dispute : gravity
    (E)   sorrow : reticence

MATCHING ANTONYMS   Answers on page 247

Knowing opposites is helpful. Match the words in column A with their antonyms in column B.

	A	B
_____	**1.** predecessor	lax
_____	**2.** affluent	malicious

_____	**3.** gravity	scan
_____	**4.** stringent	ignore
_____	**5.** resilience	heir
_____	**6.** benevolent	temerity
_____	**7.** placate	indigent
_____	**8.** peruse	silly
_____	**9.** heed	irritate
_____	**10.** judiciousness	levity
_____	**11.** profound	even-tempered
_____	**12.** irascible	rigidity

FILL IN THE BLANKS

Answers on page 247

From the choices offered below, select the word that best completes the meaning and logic of each sentence. Be sure to put each word into the correct grammatical form.

volition   tenacious   raze   obliterate
garner   reticent   virtuoso   quandary
rebuff   irrefutable   meticulous   proponent   zenith

1 A glance at Amy's trophies and you'd think her whole goal in life was to _____ swimming awards.

2 Even after several months, I'm still as _____ about the upkeep of my old used car as I was at first.

3 My friend Juan is _____ on every topic but music, the one subject that really loosens his tongue.

4 I wish that females understood how afraid guys are of being _____ when they call girls for dates.

5 A wrecking crew _____ the old theater and carted away all the debris, thus _____ all traces of the structure.

6 In Dicken's *A Tale of Two Cities*, Sydney Carton goes to the gallows of his own _____ in order to save another man's life and thereby secure a woman's happiness.

7 Our neighbors were in a _____ over what to call their new French restaurant until Dad suggested "Le Snail."

8 "Well, Meatloaf," Mom said accusingly, "these feathered corpses are _____ evidence of what you did last night!"

9 Martin Luther King was one of the most eloquent _____ of equality of opportunity for all Americans.

10 To study tennis _____ , look at some old clips of Arthur Ashe, Martina Navratilova, and John McEnroe.

11 As one who remembers everything she's read, my Aunt Jolly must have one of the world's most _____ minds.

12 Michael Jackson reached the _____ of his career at a very young age compared with most performers.

VACILLATE NOT!

acclaim • rejuvenate • revere • sanction • temper • saturate • whet • scrutinize • vacillate • thwart • venerate • waive

---

ACCLAIM v. *to proclaim or announce with noisy approval, such as shouts and applause* n. **acclaim** and **acclamation**

The first time he was in a dog show, Dude found the *acclaim* he loves. When he was *acclaimed* as Best of Breed in the Yorkshire terrier class, he strutted in front of the audience with obvious delight in their applause.

REJUVENATE v. *to make youthful or like new again; to renew or reinvigorate*

The restoration of my old secondhand car has *rejuvenated* it entirely. "You've accomplished a total *rejuvenation*," Dad told me, gazing at it with admiration.

REVERE v. *to respect and honor; to venerate, worship* n. **reverence**

For the Puritans, the words *revere, respect,* and *venerate* described much of their lives. They taught their children to *revere* God, their country, adults, and one another.

SANCTION v. *to confirm, authorize; endorse, approve, support* n. **sanction,** *authorization, approval* n. **sanctions,** *forceful measures to assure compliance with law (usu. international)*

Although Senior Skip Day is an old tradition, our principal has said, "I can't *sanction* it, although I'll probably condone it again. Obviously, no principal can *sanction* the breaking of school rules."

TEMPER v. *to moderate or adjust as conditions require; or, to strengthen through hardship*

In his inaugural address, John F. Kennedy referred to Americans as a people "*tempered* by war, disciplined

CLAM/CLAIM = to shout, cry out

clamor—*great outcry or shouting; noisy or confused demand*
> the *clamor* of his fans
> all *clamoring* for attention

disclaim—*to deny or disavow; speak in denial; repudiate*
> *disclaim* all knowledge
> file a *disclaimer* (legal denial)

Also: **acclaim, exclamation, exclaim, proclaim, proclamation, declaim, declamation, reclaim, reclamation**

by a hard and bitter peace." Forty years later, we have yet to *temper* our military needs so that we might attend to other urgent problems.

SATURATE v. *to fill completely; satiate, soak*
If I study in Spain for a college semester, I can *saturate* myself with Spanish. The best way to learn any language is by total immersion or *saturation*.

WHET v. *to excite or stimulate (the mind or appetite); to hone or sharpen (a knife or mind)*
In *Sea Fever*, poet John Masefield wrote, "I must down to the seas again, to the vagrant gypsy life, To the gull's way and the whale's way, where the wind's like a *whetted* knife." Great old poems like that *whet* everyone's appetite for more.

SCRUTINIZE v. *to examine minutely, with close attention* n. **scrutiny**, *close examination*
Now that Dude's in dog shows occasionally, we've learned to *scrutinize* him from head to tail before judging. He seems to enjoy being *scrutinized*, probably because he's so vain.

VACILLATE v. *to fluctuate; to change from one opinion to another; also, to hesitate*
"People who *vacillate* drive me right up the wall," Dad says. "I work better with definite, confident people, not folks who are *vacillating* like a bunch of dithering birds!"

90

THWART v. *to foil, baffle, or frustrate (someone's attempts)*

A young Yorky named Princess has pranced onto the show dog scene and may *thwart* Dude's chances for Best of Breed next year. Having been *thwarted* myself in wrestling matches, I know how tough it is to come in second-best.

VENERATE v. *to revere, respect, and admire with deference* adj. **venerable**, *worthy of respect*

No matter how he acted, King Henry VIII of Britain expected his subjects to *venerate* him. Today's royal family, to the open dismay of the *venerable* Elizabeth II, is forfeiting its right to *veneration* by behavior no longer overlooked.

WAIVE v. *to give up voluntarily; relinquish; forgo or postpone*

An obviously guilty student *waived* his right to a trial in student court. My family has a home court, but no one ever yields without being heard; we're all too independent to *waive* a chance at justifying our actions.

PLEX/PLIC/PLY = to fold
imply—*to suggest or hint without stating directly*
implied I ought to diet
stung by her *implication*
explicit—*fully and precisely revealed; without question*
follow her *explicit* orders
a need for you to be *explicit*
Also: **complex, complicate, comply, implication, explicate, reply, replicate, replica**

MEMORY FIX

To learn these new words, write each one on a sheet of paper. Also write a synonym or definition for each and say the words aloud as you work.

SUBSTITUTION

Answers on page 247

> **Replace each *italicized* word or phrase with the correct word from the list of words in List 11, including words from roots.**

1 "Fresh paint and wallpaper will absolutely *make like new again* this old apartment," Mom told our elderly aunt. _____

2 "Quit *shilly-shallying* and dive in," the swim coach yelled. _____

3 "Are you *hinting* that I dye my hair?" Aunt Jolly teased as she patted her bright red-orange curls. _____

4 Consideration for others' feelings sometimes causes us to *adjust as conditions demand* honesty with thoughtfulness. _____

5 After her astonishing victory in the relay, Amy was greeted with *noisy shouts of approval.* _____

6 Confucius taught his followers to *respect and honor* their elders. _____

7 Mom and Amy *carefully examined* the menu before ordering giant taco salads. _____

8 "I absolutely *refuse to acknowledge* any dog this muddy," Mom said, grinning at filthy little Dude. _____

9 A recent class debate focused on the *legal restrictions* against whaling in U.S. waters, because we can no longer *endorse or authorize* killing those endangered mammals. _____

10 A brief explanation of the case showed us why the defendant had *relinquished* his right to a trial by jury. _____

FIND THE ODDBALL   Answers on page 247

> In each word group, cross out the oddball, the one unrelated word or phrase.

1 fill up   satiate   sponge   soak   saturate

2 twist   sharpen   excite   stimulate   whet

3 thwart   flinch   frustrate   foil   baffle

4 dankness   clamor   outcry   shouting   uproar

5 implied   fully revealed   precise   explicit   unquestionable

6 defer to   venerate   honor   deter   revere

7 urge   support   authorize   endorse   sanction

8 repudiate   deny   discourage   disavow   disclaim

9 forgo   yield willingly   relinquish   relegate   waive

10 reject   inspect   scrutinize   examine   study carefully

TRUE OR FALSE Answers on page 247

> **Read each sentence to see how the words in List 11 are being used. Then mark T (true) or F (false) beside each sentence.**

1 Medication doesn't need to come with *explicit* advice. _____

2 You should *thwart* the baby's attempt to ride a tricycle down the porch steps. _____

3 It's great when your idea meets with universal *acclaim*. _____

4 Just as steel is *tempered* for strength, so are survival skills *tempered* during hard times. _____

5 Exciting previews *whet* our desire to see a movie. _____

6 Sleeping people appreciate a soothing *clamor* nearby. _____

7 Avoid being *saturated* with knowledge before exams. _____

8 You can't *rejuvenate* a dead plant you haven't watered in a month. _____

HOW MUCH IS A DEARTH?

brevity • criterion • delineate • ephemeral • copious • dearth • evanescent • paucity • prodigious • meager • redundant • scanty

BREVITY n. *shortness, briefness; conciseness of expression*
In *Hamlet* our class found this famous quotation: "*Brevity* is the soul of wit." And in Coleridge's poetry we found: "What is an Epigram? a dwarfish whole, Its body *brevity* and wit its soul." Coleridge and Shakespeare probably would have laughed at the same short jokes.

CRITERION n. *a standard used for making judgments* pl. **criteria**
After all the basic *criteria* for judging dogs have been satisfied, a judge looks for a happy, friendly dog. For pet owners, temperament is always the most important *criterion* for evaluating a dog.

DELINEATE v. *to portray accurately; outline, describe*
The guidance counselor *delineated* the various aspects of college applications. She concentrated most on the essays, with a careful *delineation* of the criteria for a good essay.

EPHEMERAL adj. *short-lived, fleeting, transient*
It's good that mosquitoes, gnats, and flies have *ephemeral* lives. But my time in high school is beginning to seem pretty *ephemeral* too, and that's not so good.

COPIOUS adj. *superabundant; in plentiful supply*
Our yard has a *copious* supply of moles, which are awfully destructive. We're waiting for Meatloaf-the-Assassin to turn that *copious* number into a dearth.

DEARTH n. *scarcity or lack; paucity*
Our class debated the poet Keats's comment on "the inhuman *dearth* of noble natures" and disagreed with

> **MIN = less, little**
>
> **minuscule**—*very, very small*
> > a *minuscule* insect
> > a pitiful, *minuscule* effort
>
> **mince**—*to chop very fine; to walk or talk in an affected way*
> > *mince* the onions
> > she *minced* her way down the aisle
>
> Also: **minus, diminish, diminution, minority, miniature**

Keats. "There's no *dearth* of good people," our teacher said, "but it's the other kind who make headlines."

EVANESCENT adj. *fading or vanishing quickly, like vapor; transient* n. **evanescence**
Ghosts are naturally *evanescent*, or so the story goes. I was a Halloween trick-or-treat ghost years ago, but a guy under a sheet isn't nearly as *evanescent* as he'd like to be.

PAUCITY n. *lack or scarcity of number or amount*

The word *paucity* is rarely used, except on SATs or PSATs. I often read about the "lack of" something or that "only a few exist," but for standardized tests, *paucity* lives on. Sigh.

PRODIGIOUS adj. *inspiring awe; enormous in size or capacity*
Dinosaurs were creatures of *prodigious* size and exotic appearance, two qualities that fascinate. Children especially have a *prodigious* appetite for facts about dinosaurs.

MEAGER adj. *lacking in quality or quantity; scanty, skimpy, spare, sparse* also, **meagre**
I have used *meager* to describe tons of things. For instance: a narrow house on a *meager* lot; an old woman, *meager* of frame and stooped; he made only a *meager* effort; and why did you give me such a *meager* amount of spaghetti when I'm starving?

REDUNDANT adj. *extra and unnecessary; superfluous; unneeded* n. **redundancy**
Redundancies are tautological expressions that drive editors nuts. For example, "young kitten" and "young

foal" are *redundant* because kitten and foal refer only to animals that are young. Also, "first and foremost" is a *redundant* expression.

MAGN = great, large

magnanimous—*generously forgiving; big-spirited*
> a *magnanimous* gesture
> the *magnanimous* nature of his soul

magnate—*someone of power, rank, or influence*
> an oil *magnate*
> the current banking *magnate*

Also: **magnify, magnificent, magnitude, magnanimity**

SCANTY adj. *brief or short; lacking desired amount or size; meager*
I thought I liked *scanty* swimsuits until I saw my girlfriend in the *scantiest* bikini in the world. I instantly became Mister Jealous Boyfriend and said she couldn't wear that *scanty* excuse for a suit where anyone else could see her.

MEMORY FIX

To learn these new words, write each one on a sheet of paper. Also write a synonym or definition for each and say the words aloud as you work.

FILL IN THE BLANKS Answers on page 237

> **From the new words in List 12, select the one that best completes the meaning and logic of each sentence. Use the correct form of the word.**

1 In order to choose a winner fairly, all contestants must be judged on the same _____ .

2 Please _____ which topics to cover in this essay.

3 Will there ever be a day when there's a _____ of problems and a _____ supply of good answers?

4 Amy _____ across the stage, self-conscious from head to toe.

5 An affluent newspaper _____ funds ten scholarships.

MATCHING Answers on page 237

> **Choose the two words or phrases that best explain the meaning of each word in bold type.**

1 **brevity**
- (A) description
- (B) briefness
- (C) humor
- (D) conciseness

2 **delineate**
- (A) draw freehand
- (B) show artistically
- (C) outline
- (D) portray accurately

3 prodigious

    (A) wasteful
    (B) immense
    (C) enormous
    (D) liberal

4 dearth

    (A) scarcity
    (B) ground
    (C) paucity
    (D) soil

5 ephemeral

    (A) fleeting
    (B) transient
    (C) beautiful
    (D) sorrowful

6 meager

    (A) narrow-minded
    (B) Tarzan growl
    (C) scanty
    (D) skimpy

7 redundant

    (A) clamorous
    (B) unnecessary
    (C) dimwitted
    (D) superfluous

8 magnanimous

    (A) generous in spirit
    (B) large rodent
    (C) uncomfortably large
    (D) big-hearted

WORDS IN CONTEXT Answers on page 248

Write the meaning of each *italicized* word on the lines provided.

1 certainly the most important *criterion* for acceptance

_____

2 wealthy oil *magnate* from the Middle East

_____

3 the *evanescent* fragrance of perfume

_____

4 a list of *copious* complaints

_____

5 only a *minuscule* amount of whipped cream

_____

6 shouldn't *mince* words with her

_____

7 enjoyed the depth and *brevity* of his talk

_____

8 King Arthur's legendary *magnanimous* nature

_____

9 numerous *redundant* sentences to be cut

_____

10 renovation demanded a *prodigious* amount of energy

_____

100

MATCHING ANTONYMS

Answers on page 248

> **In the column on the right, find two antonyms for each word at the left.**

_____ **1.** ephemeral

_____

_____ **2.** copious

_____

_____ **3.** scanty

_____

copious

scanty

meager

tiny

abundant

superabundance

_____ **4.** dearth

_____

_____ **5.** prodigious

_____

plentiful amount

enduring

minuscule

long-lived

101

LIST 13 AN ECLECTIC COLLECTION

aesthetic • eclectic • gratuitous • inevitable
• irony • expedient • apocryphal • heinous
• mundane • arduous • prodigal • quixotic

AESTHETIC adj. *referring to a sense of beauty; artistic*
Poet James Terry White recognized the importance of *aesthetic* needs, recommending that you "buy hyacinths to feed thy soul." Flowers are *aesthetically* necessary to some; others, like me, need music or time alone in a wilderness area.

ECLECTIC adj. *carefully selected from many good sources*
I have a small but *eclectic* assortment of tapes and CDs ranging from the Dead to Tchaikovsky. Amy says our house is furnished in an *eclectic* manner, but our stuff is really just a collection of hand-me-downs from a large family.

GRATUITOUS adj. *offered freely, but not necessary under the circumstances, therefore unwanted or unneeded*
I guess everyone with a big family has one relative known for *gratuitous* advice. Ours is Uncle Mort, who drops his *gratuitous* comments into every conversation.

INEVITABLE adj. *unavoidable*
Uncle Mort's steady string of helpful advice used to annoy me, but now I know it's *inevitable*. His verbal wind is just as *inevitable* as the wind outside.

IRONY n. *the opposite of what would be normal or expected; humor based on incongruity* adj. **ironic**
Mom says that the real *irony* about Uncle Mort is that he's so often right. Most *ironic* of all is his habit of being right about kids, although he has none himself.

> **LEG/LECT/LIG = to choose, pick, read**
>
> **predilection**—*natural preference; positive feelings for*
>
>   cat's *predilection* for mice
>   her *predilection* for jazz
>
> **negligible**—*of only minor importance, if any*
>   a *negligible* difference
>   his influence was *negligible*
>
> Also: **legion, legation, legible, illegible, legumes (beans and peas that are picked), eligible, select, legacy**

EXPEDIENT adj. *suitable, practical, or advisable; also, opportunistic* n. **expediency**
In history class we discussed the view that the bomb dropped on Hiroshima was an *expedient* action undertaken to end World War II. Many felt that *expediency* had obscured morality in that case, so we had a heated argument.

APOCRYPHAL adj. *of doubtful authorship; fictitious*
Highly visible or controversial people often have comments attributed to them that are *apocryphal*. Even so, *apocryphal* quotations have a habit of surviving.

HEINOUS adj. *shockingly awful, appalling; abominable, outrageous*
Cult leaders Jim Jones and David Koresh led their followers into death, thereby committing a *heinous* crime: murder. Mass murder of trusting people is as *heinous* as anything I can imagine.

MUNDANE adj. *everyday, commonplace, like menial chores*
As the opposite of celestial or heavenly, anything *mundane* should be dull, but it isn't always. Washing the car is a *mundane* chore, but I like slopping around on a wet driveway.

ARDUOUS adj. *demanding, hard to achieve; strenuous*

Packing gear into a wilderness camping area seems *arduous* to some, but not to me and my friends. For my friend Rob, writing an essay is an *arduous* job.

PRODIGAL adj. *wildly extravagant or lavish in spending*

LEG = law

legitimate—*correct by law; conforming to accepted procedure*
> a *legitimate* driver
> a logical, *legitimate* reason

legislate—*to formally enact as law; to rule legally*
> a recently *legislated* statute
> our state *legislature*

Also: **legal, illegal, legitimize, legate** *(official emissary)*

Mom and Dad don't talk about our government's *prodigal* spending; they yell. They feel strongly about using funds wisely, so none of us is *prodigal* with money.

QUIXOTIC adj. *extravagantly idealistic; unpredictable; unrealistic or imaginary*
The word *quixotic* comes from the character Don Quixote in Cervantes's novel, a story of a lovable, wacky old fellow who imagines that he's a knight. *Quixotic* ideas are strange, a little crazy, but often wonderful.

MEMORY FIX
To learn these new words, write each one on a sheet of paper. Also write a synonym or definition for each and say the words aloud as you work.

MATCHING Answers on page 238

> **Match the words in column A with their meanings in column B and write the meanings in the spaces provided.**

	A	B
_____	**1.** gratuitous	opportunistic
_____	**2.** inevitable	insanely idealistic
_____	**3.** expedient	abominable, appalling
_____	**4.** arduous	commonplace
_____	**5.** quixotic	unwanted or unneeded
_____	**6.** apocryphal	strenuous
_____	**7.** mundane	unavoidable
_____	**8.** heinous	of doubtful authorship

FILL IN THE BLANKS Answers on page 238

> **From the words below, select the one that best completes the meaning and logic of this essay.**

aesthetic   ironic   predilection   negligible
eclectic   prodigal   legislate   legitimate

Meatloaf's undisguised _____ for small, furry
(1)
critters results in many "gifts" left on the porch for our
family. Last year's presents from Meatloaf were a(n)
_____ array of mice, moles, birds, and shrews. In
(2)
the summer, Meatloaf was absolutely _____ with
(3)
these offerings, which we found pretty gross as time
went on.

"There's no _____ reason for her to hunt."
(4)
Mom fumed. "We feed her enough that she could

105

ignore her cat instincts!" Both Mom and Amy wish we could _____ a cat's behavior, but cats adhere
(5)
strictly to their own laws.

"No point in scolding. Anything you say to a cat has only a _____ effect on its behavior," Dad
(6)
observed. "How _____ that we should love a
(7)
hunter," he went on, "when we're such fervent pacifists."

Of course, the grace and beauty of cats appeal to the _____ senses of many people, not just to our
(8)
family.

Choose the one word pair in each list below that expresses the same relationship as the pair in capital letters.

1 DAYDREAMING : QUIXOTIC
- (A) bicycling : expedient
- (B) giving : prodigal
- (C) reading : legitimate
- (D) cleaning house : mundane
- (E) eating : aesthetic

2 BAD : HEINOUS
- (A) gratuitous : free
- (B) aesthetic : artistic
- (C) prodigal : scanty
- (D) proposed : legitimate
- (E) difficult : arduous

3 APOCRYPHAL : LEGEND

    (A) long-range : goal
    (B) fictitious : fable
    (C) inevitable : story
    (D) gratuitous : gossip
    (E) hero : prodigal

FIND THE ANTONYM Answers on page 238

> **Pair the words below with their antonyms by writing them on the correct lines.**

parsimonious	haphazard	significant	apocryphal
aversion	quixotic	customary	mundane
noble	desired	avoidable	impractical

_____ **1.** authentic

_____ **2.** sensible

_____ **3.** inevitable

_____ **4.** gratuitous

_____ **5.** negligible

_____ **6.** predeliction

_____ **7.** eclectic

_____ **8.** heinous

_____ **9.** ironic

_____ **10.** heavenly

_____ **11.** prodigal

_____ **12.** expedient

YAKKETY YAK

---

verbose • blasphemy • vilify • diatribe • vitriolic • jargon • satire • tirade • slander • garble • rhetoric • garrulous

---

VERBOSE adj. *using more words than necessary; wordy*
When the teacher writes *VERBOSE!* across the top of my paper, I know I got carried away with descriptions again. The sin of *verbosity* is shared by many writers, of course, Stephen King included.

BLASPHEMY n. *disrespect or irreverence toward something sacred or seriously important* n. **blaspheme**
Playwright George Bernard Shaw wrote in *Pygmalion*, "Independence? That's middle-class *blasphemy*. We are all dependent on one another, every soul of us on earth." And later he said, "All great truths begin as *blasphemies*."

VILIFY v. *to slander or defame someone's name or standing in the community; to malign* n. **vilification**
The tabloid papers you see in the grocery store will apparently *vilify* anyone in public life. Their *vilifications* of prominent figures make me shake my head and wonder.

DIATRIBE n. *bitter, critical speech or writing*
Diatribes flourish in politics, where people seem eager to criticize others. Negative, name-calling speeches were banned in our school elections so that anything resembling a *diatribe* was cut short.

VITRIOLIC adj. *burning or corrosive like acid; caustic*
Political activists sometimes give *vitriolic* speeches when they're trying to make a point. But hearing these emotional, *vitriolic* attacks usually turns me against the speaker.

> **QUER/QUIR/QUIS = to ask, seek**
>
> **querulous—***complaining, fault-finding, fretful; petulant*
> > a *querulous* tone of voice
> > her repeated, *querulous* comments
>
> **inquisitive—***inquiring, questioning, curious*
> > an *inquisitive* mind
> > an *inquisitive* sort of person
>
> Also: **acquire, acquisition, query, inquire, require, inquisition, perquisite** *(perk),* **exquisite, requisition, requisite**

JARGON n. *special language or terminology; dialect or hybrid language*
Every industry or specialty develops its own *jargon*—words and expressions that only the insiders know. Kids often develop a *jargon* that sets them apart from their parents.

SATIRE n. *comedy using laughter as a weapon to evoke a feeling of scorn along with amusement*
My history class is reading *Huckleberry Finn*, Twain's *satire* that ridicules the prejudice, stupidity, and hypocrisy in America in the mid-nineteenth century. Twain's insightful *satiric* pen gives us laughter along with truth.

TIRADE n. *a lengthy, emotional, critical speech*
Coaches tend to lapse into a *tirade* when a team player makes a serious mistake. For those who have to listen to them, *tirades* are extremely memorable.

SLANDER n. *a false, defamatory spoken criticism of someone* v. *to defame with untrue speech*
While libel is only written, *slander* refers to nasty, personal criticism that is only oral. Both libel and *slander* can be grounds for a lawsuit.

GARBLE n. *to change or alter meaning through misrepresentation of facts or distortion of ideas*
If you want to *garble* a message, just play telephone as you did at kids' birthday parties. One *garbled* message I remember began as "Who's Superman?" and ended up "Where's Pooh's can?"

RHETORIC n. *insincere or high-flown writing or speech; originally, the study of good communication*

DIC/DICT = to speak, say; words

indict—*to charge with an offense, in court or informally*

> *indicted* for the crime of murder
> *indicted* by my own family

edict—*a formal order or command; a command by law*

> Mom's *edict* on bedtime
> the governor's latest *edict*

Also: **dictate, predict, indicate, indicative, dictatorial, dictionary, dictaphone, dictator, predicate**

Rhetoric has degenerated from something admirable and worthy of study to something contemptible, as when we accuse someone of "mere *rhetoric*." A *rhetorical* question is one asked for effect, with little hope of a serious answer.

GARRULOUS adj. *extremely talkative, gabby, loquacious, verbose* n. **garrulity**

Our Aunt Jolly is pretty *garrulous*, but we enjoy her verbosity because it's funny and never cruel. *Garrulity*

turns people off if it drones on in a negative, critical way.

MEMORY FIX

Again, to learn these new words, write each one on a sheet of paper. Also write a synonym or definition for each and say the words aloud as you work.

SUBSTITUTION   Answers on page 249

> **Replace each *italicized* word or phrase with the correct word from List 14, including words from roots.**

1 The teacher explained the assignment by asking several *just-for-effect* questions to get us thinking.

_____

2 Don't *badly interpret* that information, please.

_____

3 His talk wasn't a lecture, it was a *bitter, critical speech* on the evils of drinking. _____

4 Jonathan Swift's most biting *comedy arousing scorn* was "A Modest Proposal," in which he suggested a grisly solution to the Irish famine. _____

5 "Have some dessert?" shrieked Amy. "When you know I'm dieting? That's *an unthinkable insult or disrespect*!" _____

6 Gabbing throughout dinner and the movie is one sure way to get yourself described as *extremely talkative*. _____

7 It's taking Mom and Dad a while to learn the *special language* that goes with computers. _____

8 After hearing the evidence, the jury *formally charged* the suspect on a charge of grand larceny. _____

9 As we watched the movie, I felt my youngest cousin grow tense during the evil Queen's *lengthy, emotional speech* against innocent Snow White. _____

10 Respectable news stations are careful not to air *material that would damage someone's reputation*. _____

TRUE OR FALSE Answers on page 239

> **Read each sentence to see if it is correct. Then mark T (true) or F (false) beside each.**

1 If you want folks to think you're a rocket scientist, you'll need a bit of rocketry *jargon*. _____

2 If people in the audience say, "Hmm, more *rhetoric*," at the end of your speech, you'll feel proud. _____

3 When you're asking Dad if you can borrow the car, a *vitriolic* tone will probably work the best. _____

4 Swearing is unacceptable *blasphemy* to many people. _____

5 The cartoon strip *Doonesbury* uses *satire* to good advantage. _____

6 A *querulous* "Why aren't you up?" starts the day right. _____

7 Truly vicious *slander* can *vilify* a person almost beyond redemption. _____

MATCHING Answers on page 239

> From the column on the right, select two
> synonyms or phrases that explain each of the
> words at the left and write in your answers.

_____	**1.** verbose	corrosive
_____		petulant
_____	**2.** vilify	wordy
_____		questioning
_____	**3.** querulous	defame
_____		legal order
_____	**4.** vitriolic	command
_____		malign
_____	**5.** edict	slander
_____		caustic
_____	**6.** inquisitive	curious
_____		garrulous
_____	**7.** slander	dishonor
_____		fretful

www.petersons.com

WISHY-WASHY

---

ambiguous • capitulate • defer • ambivalence • dubious • languor • fluctuate • tentative • indifferent • lethargy • innocuous • stagnant

---

AMBIGUOUS adj. *indefinite, open to more than one interpretation; obscure, uncertain* n. **ambiguity**
When Mom asked if the snake was loose in the house, I gave an *ambiguous* reply to keep her from worrying. But Mom hates *ambiguity*, and she said, "Yes or no? Be definite!"

CAPITULATE v. *to give in, surrender, acquiesce*
I *capitulated* under pressure and admitted that the snake was somewhere in the house. I begged Mom to stay in her room until we'd found him, and she *capitulated* readily.

DEFER v. *to yield to someone of greater authority or age; to put off until another time* n. **deference**
After finding the snake wrapped around the warm coils of the refrigerator, we *deferred* to Mom's wishes and moved him to the garage. I can no longer *defer* making him a stout cage.

AMBIVALENCE n. *fluctuation between one thing and another; uncertainty or indecision*
People are rarely *ambivalent* about snakes; either they like them or not. Mom hasn't any *ambivalence* about them whatever and thinks they all belong in zoos.

DUBIOUS adj. *doubtful; of questionable truth or quality; suspicious*
Unfortunately, Mom regards my fondness for wildlife as a *dubious* character trait. When I adopted a box turtle, she said he was of *dubious* value as a pet.

LANGUOR n. *sluggishness; tiredness or weakness; lethargy* adj. **languid**
Cats are *languorous* animals, stretching and yawning sleepily in the sun, then flopping down to doze again.

VAD/VAS = to go

evade—*to avoid, dodge, or circumvent a person or issue*

> *evaded* the issue
> *evaded* detection
> her *evasive* answer

pervade—*to go throughout, to diffuse throughout, to permeate*

> hint of fear *pervaded* the room
> a *pervasive* odor of skunk

Also: **evasion, invade, invasion, pervasion**

This *languor* is true of cats of all types; cats sleep more hours a day than most other animals.

FLUCTUATE v. *to shift up and down; or, to come and go, as ocean waves*

Newscasters report daily *fluctuations* in the stock market, in temperatures, and in public opinion on current topics. Emotions *fluctuate* too, of course, according to what's happening in our lives.

TENTATIVE adj. *hesitant, unsure, uncertain*

E. B. White, author of *Charlotte's Web* and coauthor of *The Elements of Style*, warns us about *tentative* writing. "Vigorous writing is concise," he says, "and definite." Prose hedged with qualifiers is not only *tentative*, of course, it's also more wordy.

INDIFFERENT adj. *not good or bad; unconcerned or not curious; aloof or detached; unbiased*

An *indifferent* student doesn't care about learning. Someone who regards flowers with an *indifferent* eye isn't interested in flowers. *Indifference* can extend all the way to total detachment.

LETHARGY n. *serious tiredness; languor, laziness, torpor*

The *lethargy* of cats is rooted in their physiological need for sleep because of hearts and lungs proportionately smaller than those of other animals. When on a chase, though, the *lethargic* cheetah is the fastest critter on land.

INNOCUOUS adj. *harmless; or, dull, insipid*

The school's play director said he was tired of doing safe, *innocuous* plays. This year's play may cause a few raised eyebrows, but it certainly isn't *innocuous*.

DUC/DUCT = to lead, direct
deduce—*to conclude or infer by reasoned thought*
   deduce that from the evidence
   a clever *deduction*
conducive—*apt to promote or assist*
   atmosphere *conducive* to learning
   a bed *conducive* to rest
Also: **induce, induction, reduce, reduction, seduce, seduction, conduct, conduction, abduct, deduct**

STAGNANT adj. *unmoving or not flowing (stagnant water); stale (stagnant air); inactive* v. **stagnate**
We've all seen *stagnant* ponds and met people who have let their minds *stagnate*. A new word was born about twenty years ago when *stagnation* married *inflation* and created *stagflation*, an economic term describing stubborn inflation blended with *stagnant* consumer demand and noticeable unemployment.

MEMORY FIX
And again . . . hang in there and write each new word and a synonym or definition for each. Say the words aloud as you write them.

WORDS IN CONTEXT Answers on page 249

Write the meaning of each *italicized* word based on how it is used in its quotation.

1 George Bernard Shaw: "The worst sin towards our fellow creatures is not to hate them, but to be *indifferent* to them: that's the essence of inhumanity."

_____

2 Samuel Johnson: "I will be conquered; I will not *capitulate*." _____

3 Francis Bacon: "*Defer* not charities till death."

_____

4 President Grover Cleveland: "After an existence of nearly 20 years of almost *innocuous* desuetude [disuse] these laws are brought forth."

_____

5 Percy Bysshe Shelley, "To A Skylark":
"With thy clear keen joyance
Languor cannot be." _____

6 William Wordsworth, "National Independence and Liberty":
"Milton! thou shouldst be living at this hour:
England hath need of thee; she is a fen
Of *stagnant* waters."

7 Sir Isaac Newton, ". . . whatever is not *deduced* from the phenomena is to be called an hypothesis." _____

MATCHING   Answers on page 239

Choose the two words or phrases that best explain the meaning of each word in bold type.

1 **fluctuate**
(A) vary up or down
(B) group together in a flock
(C) disturb
(D) come and go

2 **dubious**
(A) old musical refrain
(B) suspicious
(C) of doubtful quality
(D) sneaky

117

3 ambivalence

(A) versatility
(B) medical vehicle
(C) wishy-washiness
(D) indecision

4 tentative

(A) hesitant
(B) unsure
(C) camping term
(D) timely

5 lethargic

(A) revolting
(B) languorous
(C) sick
(D) torpid

6 ambiguous

(A) two-faced
(B) enlarged
(C) indefinite
(D) uncertain

7 evade

(A) avoid
(B) hide
(C) circumvent
(D) fool

8 conducive

(A) rewarding
(B) promoting
(C) punishing
(D) assisting

9 pervade

(A) become weird
(B) dole out
(C) permeate
(D) diffuse throughout

118

FIND THE SYNONYM

Answers on page 249

> From the choices offered below, select the missing synonym for each word group and write it in the space provided.

capitulate   stagnant   defer   innocuous
languor   tentative   evade   indifferent

1 dodge   avoid   circumvent   be elusive

_____

2 yield in respect   postpone   suspend   put off

_____

3 sluggishness   weariness   torpor   lethargy

_____

4 dull   harmless   insipid   inoffensive

_____

5 stale   motionless   inactive   not flowing

_____

6 unconcerned   detached   not curious   aloof

_____

7 hesitant   undeveloped   unsure   uncertain

_____

8 give in   yield   acquiesce   surrender

_____

119

REVIEW: LISTS 11–15

Quick, quick, a handy review before those new words have a chance to slip away. To begin, read over lists 11–15. Say each word and its meaning aloud.

ANALOGIES Answers on page 239

Choose the one word pair in each list below that expresses the same relationship as the pair in capital letters.

1 VACILLATE : AMBIVALENCE

(A) disclaim : legitimacy
(B) whet : garrulity
(C) blaspheme : irreverence
(D) delineate : truth
(E) indict : suspect

2 EPHEMERAL : DURATION

(A) scanty : apparel
(B) negligible : interest
(C) inevitable : weather
(D) meager : amount
(E) minuscule : portion

3 SATIRE : IRONY

(A) comedy : tragedy
(B) tirade : criticism
(C) rhetoric : politics
(D) diatribe : speech
(E) paucity : emotion

4 REPUTATION : SLANDER

(A) predilection : favor
(B) inquisition : demand
(C) sanction : grant
(D) indictment : announce
(E) communication : garble

5 SPIRIT : MAGNANIMOUS

(A) criterion : first
(B) effort : prodigious
(C) edict : quixotic
(D) verbosity : redundant
(E) dearth : innocuous

MATCHING Answers on page 250

> Choose the one synonym or definition that best
> defines each word in bold type.

1 defer

(A) pine tree
(B) give way to
(C) reduce in rank
(D) abhor

2 imply

(A) hint
(B) infer
(C) layer
(D) insult

3 thwart

(A) confuse
(B) harm
(C) foil
(D) evade

4 whet

(A) urge
(B) illiterate pronoun
(C) dampen
(D) sharpen

5 predilection

(A) natural preference
(B) hasty decision
(C) garbled speech
(D) campaign jitters

6 arduous

(A) complex
(B) demanding
(C) dubious
(D) heartfelt

7 **apocryphal**

   (A) expeditious

   (B) fictitious

   (C) suspicious

   (D) Aloysius

8 **lethargy**

   (A) illness

   (B) slowness

   (C) paucity

   (D) langour

9 **explicit**

   (A) outside the law

   (B) overextended

   (C) beyond question

   (D) aboveboard

10 **redundant**

   (A) superfluous

   (B) exceedingly stupid

   (C) evanescent

   (D) backward

FIND THE ODDBALL   Answers on page 250

> **In each word group, cross out the oddball, the one unrelated word or phrase.**

1 applaud   greet with cheers   acclaim approve of   announce

2 strengthen   harden   moderate   temper   adjudicate

3 defer to   venerate   revere   admonish   respect

4 speech   brevity   conciseness   succinctness pithiness

5 garrulous   loquacious   verbose   jargon   gabbiness

6 dirty   appalling   abominable   shockingly awful   heinous

7 worklike   everyday   commonplace   menial
mundane

8 transient   ephemeral   vanishing fast
vapor   evanescent

9 open to question   dubious   suspicious
doubtful   unreal

10 slightly wacko   idealistic   goal-oriented
quixotic

11 dearth   lack   supply   paucity   scarcity
scantiness

12 whiny   querulous   petulant   fretful   adorable

FILL IN THE BLANKS Answers on page 250

> From the choices offered below, select the word
> that best completes the meaning and logic of
> each sentence. Alter the word as needed to fit the
> sentence.

copious	saturate	prodigal	clamor	pervasive
deduce	waive	negligible	vilify	eclectic
prodigious	aesthetic	diatribe	conducive	vitriolic
capitulate	fluctuate	innocuous	tentative	

1 "The students who taught this unit are writing the
quiz," said the history teacher. "I _____ all
control over it."

2 The first question was tough, so I jotted a(n)
_____ answer in the margin and decided to
come back to it later.

123

3 Sitting by the window is _____ to thoughts of canoe trips and camping, but not to recalling facts for this test.

4 Getting ready for our yearly winter campout requires careful planning, shopping, and _____ amounts of food because the guys in our group are _____ eaters.

5 We don't let Arturo shop for groceries anymore because he was a _____ spender who bought everything in sight.

6 Although Arturo nearly bankrupted us, we really pigged out on the _____ assortment of groceries he'd purchased.

7 The wilderness of pines and piercingly blue skies in winter appeals to my _____ senses.

8 Last year the temperatures on our trip _____ from below 0 at night to the high 30s in the daytime, and there was only a _____ amount of snow.

9 Although we adjusted to the _____ smell of mink that slowly permeated camp, we never _____ where it came from.

10 After a bear raided the food we thought we'd hoisted out of reach, James launched into a furious, _____ speech that _____ all bears. (I'll bet their ears are still burning.)

11 We ordered James to end the _____ , and he eventually _____ , subsiding into a fairly mumbling as he accused the bears of lying in wait for us each year.

12 With the food mostly gone, our gear _____ with the gamy odor of mink, and our bodies _____ for burgers and hot showers, we packed up and went home to civilization.

LIST 16 MORE VERBS TO LOVE

undermine • repudiate • enhance • hamper • expedite • relegate • emulate • squander • rescind • solicit • emanate • extricate

UNDERMINE v. *to weaken or destroy bit by bit; to sap the strength of by undercutting*
Nothing *undermines* your image like having a little brother tag along wherever you go. Eddie has been slowly *undermining* my patience too, ever since he learned to walk.

REPUDIATE v. *to disown, disclaim, reject, or refuse*
Of course, I always *repudiate* Eddie's determined efforts to follow me. He keeps tracking me like a shadow, however, despite my repeated, stubborn *repudiation.*

ENHANCE v. *to make better or more desirable in some way*
One day, I figured I'd *enhance* my chances of losing him if I ducked into a dark alley. Unfortunately, that idea only *enhanced* his interest in following me.

HAMPER v. *to get in the way of; to hinder or impede*
How could I *hamper* my dogged little pest? He was certainly *unhampered* by the evil eye I kept giving him.

EXPEDITE v. *to smooth or speed up a process; facilitate*
To *expedite* Eddie's departure, I offered him a dollar for ice cream. No way, I was told. As usual, some things just cannot be *expedited*, no matter what you try.

RELEGATE v. *to put away or aside; to shift to a less important place; to position by rank*
I thought about *relegating* my brother to a Pests' Dungeon, where he could never annoy me again, but I

> **JUG/JUNCT/JOIN = to join or to marry**
>
> **subjugate**—*to subdue or conquer* (lit. *"under the yoke"*)
>> *subjugated* the wildest one
>> can't *subjugate* the weather
>
> **enjoin**—*to command or order urgently; to forbid or prohibit*
>> *enjoined* by tradition from participating
>
> Also: **conjugal, conjugate, junction, conjunction, juncture, join, adjoin, rejoinder, injunction**

relegated that idea to the back of my mind as I watched his bike suddenly swerve toward the street.

EMULATE v. *to try to equal (or even exceed) an example; to imitate* n. **emulation**
He was trying to *emulate* me by popping wheelies as he'd seen me do in our driveway. I yelled, "Cut it out, twerp!" because my example was the wrong one to *emulate*.

SQUANDER v. *to use up or spend in an overgenerous or silly way; to dissipate or waste*

Startled by my yell, Eddie rammed his bike into a lamppost, and we *squandered* an hour trying to straighten his wheel. I had planned to *squander* the day in a much more enjoyable way than that, hanging out with my friends.

RESCIND v. *to cancel or annul; to repeal, call back*
"I wish I could *rescind* your right to be my brother," I grumbled, sweating over his crumpled bike. It was a mean remark, but I was too angry to *rescind* it at the time.

SOLICIT v. *to ask for time, money, or moral support; to lure into wrongdoing* adj. **solicitous,** *showing concern*
When I cooled down, I *solicitously* asked if he was okay after his scary adventure. The look I got in reply made me feel as dumb as the guy who tried to *solicit* donations of ice for Eskimos.

EMANATE v. *to seep forth (smells or ideas); to emit*
Fists balled at his sides, Eddie glared at me and *emanated* anger. My own fury dwindled as I saw how small and hurt he was. The noise of the streets

engulfed us, and cars and buses *emanated* their foul odors as we confronted each other.

TORT/TORS = to twist, wring

tortuous—*winding or twisted, like a road; crooked, tricky*
> a *tortuous* path up the hillside
> a *tortuous* thought process

extort—*to get something from a person by using fear or force or unfair power; to obtain by intimidation*
> *extorted* the information from him

Also: **retort, distort, torsion, torque, torture, torturous** (*cruel, like torture*), **tort** (*in law, a wrongful act*)

EXTRICATE v. *to free from an entanglement or awkward spot*
Eventually we got on our bikes, only to stop a few minutes later while Eddie *extricated* his shoelace from his bike gear. As I watched him, I finally accepted the fact that I'd never *extricate* myself from my little brother.

MEMORY FIX

Once more, write these words down and say each one aloud as you write its synonym or definition.

FILL IN THE BLANKS   Answers on page 250

> From the list below, select the word that best completes the meaning and logic of each phrase. Alter the words as needed to be grammatically correct.

extricate	undermine	subjugate	extort
solicitous	relegate	emanate	rescind
emulate	expedite	enhance	enjoin

1 a bylaw that _____ anyone but club members from voting

2 found his authority _____ by their growing criticism

3 put in jail for _____ money from small shopkeepers

4 watching over the sick child with _____ eyes

5 heavenly smell that _____ each spring from honeysuckle

6 old order that was _____ and taken off the books

7 fly will never _____ himself from the spider's web

8 difficult, if not impossible, to _____ Jefferson's achievements

9 carefully printed address will _____ delivery

10 historical habit of the arrogant of _____ others less aggressive

11 _____ that old chair to the basement until it's fixed

12 ready sense of humor that _____ any personality

RHYME TIME

Answers on page 250

> **Choose the correct word from List 16 for each blank in this truly corny poetry.**

1 Our woeful human tendency to hate,

I would like to and I do _____ !

2 If I tell you not to _____ ,

that means don't apply a damper

to my one essential whim.

For I won't be _____

to the group whose lives are fated

to be meaningless or grim.

3 I'll _____ my invitation to the dance,

Unless you _____ the look of those pants!

4 Will and Orville were told not to _____

Their time by aiming up yonder.

But they wanted to fly,

So they gave it a try.

Of the outcome, we couldn't be fonder.

5 I'm obliged to report

That your attempt to _____

A confession from this dope

Is a prospect without hope.

MATCHING   Answers on page 250

> **Match the words in column A with their synonyms or definitions in column B and write them down in the space provided.**

	A		B
_____	1. expedite		tortuous
_____	2. dissipate		weaken gradually
_____	3. solicit		repeal
_____	4. hinder		forbid
_____	5. undermine		try to equal
_____	6. emanate		squander
_____	7. enjoin		ask for
_____	8. emulate		hamper
_____	9. twisted		facilitate
_____	10. rescind		seep out

131

LIST 17 AN ESTEEMED ASSORTMENT

esteem • disparity • catharsis • anomaly • censure • antithesis • fallacy • indolence • fledgling • hindrance • clemency • jeopardy

ESTEEM n. *high opinion of one's worth or character* v. **esteem,** *to value extremely*
Because the British are known to *esteem* royalty, English diarist Samuel Pepys (pronounced "peeps") jokingly wrote this about King Charles II: "Methought it lessened my *esteem* of a king, that he should not be able to command the rain."

DISPARITY n. *difference in type, quality, or quantity* adj. **disparate**
Although we think there's a *disparity* between passion and reason, the English poet John Donne blended them in his poetry. After all, the perceived *disparity* between love and hate is believed to be two sides of one coin.

CATHARSIS n. *a cleansing or purging that releases emotions* adj. **cathartic**
A funeral is meant to be a *cathartic* event that allows us to vent our grief openly and fully so that it is no longer a burden. Tears are one obvious form of *catharsis*, of course.

ANOMALY n. *something different from the norm; irregularity or paradox* adj. **anomalous**
As a night owl, I'm an *anomaly* in a family of early risers who turn into pumpkins at 10 p.m. An irregularity of any kind usually sticks out, like the *anomalous* black sheep.

CENSURE n. *stern or official condemnation* v. **censure**
"No man can justly *censure* or condemn another," wrote the seventeenth-century English physician Sir Thomas Browne, "because indeed no man truly knows

> **GREG = crowd, flock, group**
>
> **gregarious**—*social and convivial; fond of groups*
> > her bubbly, *gregarious* personality
> > the *gregarious* elephant
>
> **egregious**—*painfully noticeable; flagrant; outstandingly bad*
> > *egregious* error
> > disciplined the child's *egregious* behavior
>
> Also: **congregate, congregation, aggregate, segregate**

another." Yes, but what would the media do without *censure*?

ANTITHESIS n. *a direct opposite* adj. **antithetical**
The world has lots of "near opposites," but truly *antithetical* things are rare. War is the *antithesis* of peace, day the *antithesis* of night, and good the *antithesis* of evil.

FALLACY n. *incorrect idea; wrong assumption; an error* adj. **fallacious**
The idea behind the "pathetic *fallacy*" is that when you're under severe emotional strain, you're easy prey to *fallacious* impressions. For example, it's a *fallacy* to believe that nature rejoices along with you, just because you are happy.

INDOLENCE n. *supreme laziness or idleness; sloth*
Mom's last vacation was a study in *indolence*, as she put it. "I'm majoring in sloth this week, and I refuse to even move in that direction," she said, waving one *indolent* hand toward the kitchen.

FLEDGLING n. *a young bird with new flight feathers; an untested beginner; novice*
Every field has its *fledglings*—people who have the knowledge or equipment for a job but haven't yet proved themselves. Most *fledglings* are marked by an appealing enthusiasm.

HINDRANCE n. *an obstacle, impediment; something in the way* v. **hinder**, *to impede*
At leaf-raking time, Dude becomes a real *hindrance*. He darts wildly into our tidy leaf piles, scattering leaves everywhere and *hindering* the entire project of fall cleanup.

133

NOV/NEO = new

novel—*new or original*
innovate—*to do something new*
> a *novel* idea
> *novel* solution
> a highly *innovative* plan

neophyte—*novice, beginner, tyro, newcomer, proselyte*
> a *neophyte* on the court
> fresh ideas from our *neophyte*

Also: **novelty, novice, novitiate, renovate, neon, neonatal, neologism**

CLEMENCY n. *lenience or moderation in punishment; mercy* adj. **clement,** *mild (weather); merciful*
In *The Merchant of Venice*, Portia asks that justice be tempered with *clemency* for Antonio, who owes Shylock a pound of flesh. That famous soliloquy seeking a *clement* judgment begins, "The quality of mercy is not strain'd, It droppeth as the gentle rain from heaven. . . ."

JEOPARDY n. *an exposure to or possibility of danger*
Jeopardy began as the Latin phrase *jocus partitus*, tied game, then became French, *jeu parti*, meaning that the game's outcome was uncertain. Now when people are in *jeopardy* they are at risk or even in serious danger—except on the program of that name, which is still a game.

MEMORY FIX

Quick, take out a piece of paper and write down each of these new words along with a definition.

134

TRUE OR FALSE Answers on page 250

> **Read each sentence to see how the words in List 17 are being used. Then mark T (true) or F (false) beside each.**

1 Any business is managed best by a *neophyte*. _____

2 Acquiring knowledge helps to build *self-esteem*. _____

3 Repeated *censure* destroys self-esteem. _____

4 Rage is the *antithesis* of anger. _____

5 A stew is typically made from *disparate* ingredients. _____

6 There are noticeable *disparities* between identical twins. _____

7 The most prized assistant is an *indolent* one. _____

8 It's tough to hide an *anomaly* in the herd. Likewise, an *anomaly* in the herd had better have a tough hide. _____

9 When sad or depressed, spending time with comics Robin Williams and Billy Crystal might be very *cathartic*. _____

10 Thinking that I'll be a good diver because I'm a good swimmer is probably *fallacious* reasoning. _____

FIND THE ODDBALL Answers on page 240

In each word group below, cross out the oddball—the one unrelated word or phrase.

1 regard   value   prize   outlook   esteem

2 honor   merciful   forgiving   lenient   indulgent

3 strong disapproval   urgency   condemnation   censure

4 symbiosis   antonymous pair   opposition   antithesis

5 master   tyro   neophyte   novice   fledgling   proselyte

6 original   different   novel   fresh   hackneyed

7 sociable   convivial   aloof   social   gregarious

MATCHING Answers on page 240

Find two synonyms or phrases in column B that explain each word in column A.

A	B
	sociable
1. indolence	
	obstacle
	paradox
2. clemency	
	a purging
3. catharsis	lenience
	error
4. fallacy	neophyte
	idleness

_____ **5.** hindrance   a cleansing

_____   convivial

_____ **6.** anomaly   mercy

_____   flagrant

_____ **7.** fledgling   sloth

_____   irregularity

_____ **8.** gregarious   outstandingly bad

_____   novice

_____ **9.** novel   wrong assumption

_____   original

_____ **10.** egregious   impediment

_____   new

LIST 18 FEELING GOOD

benign • blithe • elation • appease • jocular
• effervescent • extol • placid • ameliorate •
serene • frivolous • assuage

BENIGN adj. *gentle, gracious, kind; benevolent in outlook; mild or favorable, not malignant*
The dermatologist smiled *benignly* and urged me to relax. "The results of the biopsies show that the moles we removed from your hand were *benign*, not malignant, Ted."

BLITHE adj. *cheerful, lighthearted; or, casual or heedless*
A while back, I strolled in around 2 a.m. from a party, whistling *blithely*, only to meet my parents in the kitchen. They were waiting up for me, and the look on their faces was anything but *blithe*.

ELATION n. *exultation; high spirits* v. **elate**
When I saw those furious faces, my *elation* quickly faded, and I felt myself turning red. I have turned red other times, when I was exercising hard or *elated* over something, but this was a different red altogether.

APPEASE v. *to quiet, calm, allay; to pacify or conciliate (refers to people or emotions, not conditions)*
I knew it was time to *appease* the folks, and in a hurry. I choose the truth because it was my only hope, as I saw it, of *appeasing* their anger.

JOCULAR adj. *jolly, fond of joking (L. joc = joke);* also, **jocose** *and* **jocund** = *merry, witty*
My folks are *jocular* people. Dad has even called home in the middle of the day to relate some *jocose* remark from a friend at work.

EFFERVESCENT adj. *bubbling with high spirits; exhilarated* v. **to effervesce** n. **effervescence**

> **AM = to love; friend**
>
> **amiable**—*easy to get along with; friendly and good-natured*
>> a spaniel's gentle, *amiable* nature
>> an *amiable* settlement
>
> **amity**—*friendship and good-will; harmony*
>> a nation known for *amity*
>> the natural *amity* of old friends
>
> Also: **amicable, enamored, amorous, amatory, amateur, paramour**

Mom's usually an *effervescent* person, bubbling over with enthusiasm about one thing or another. It's hard to resist anybody whose spirit *effervesces* like that.

EXTOL v. *to "sing" the praises of, glorify, praise highly*

I don't usually *extol* the virtues of my parents, but when I meet other kids' folks, I know I am luckier than most. Of course, my folks *extol* their terrific kids all the time, but you expect that of parents.

PLACID v. *calm in nature, not easily ruffled; quiet, serene*

I am quieter than my parents, not *placid* exactly, but not always joking around either. My friend Greg is so *placid* that people often wonder if he's asleep.

AMELIORATE v. *to improve or better (a condition)*

Anyway, to return to the night of the Big Bad Late Party, I was able to *ameliorate* the whole sticky situation by explaining to my folks that I'd met the perfect woman. Telling the truth doesn't always *ameliorate* a problem, but it's amazing how it has repeatedly helped me.

SERENE adj. *extremely quiet, calm, and peaceful*

As I explained about meeting Beth, I saw Mom lean back against the kitchen wall and relax, gradually becoming more *serene*. She wasn't totally calm, not Mrs. *Serenity*-of-the-year or anything, but she was definitely calmer.

FRIVOLOUS adj. *not serious; inappropriately high-spirited; foolishly self-indulgent* n. **frivolity**

139

When I finished talking, Dad said, "Thanks, Ted. I wasn't in the mood for any *frivolous* excuses." I smiled, because at two in the morning he has never been in the mood for anything, let alone something *frivolous*!

PATH/PASS = feeling, suffering, disease

apathy—*lack of feeling or interest; impassiveness; indifference*
> an *apathetic* nod
> unfortunate *apathy* toward the poor

dispassionate—*fair; not affected by strong feeling*
> a *dispassionate* opinion
> a carefully *dispassionate* review

Also: **sympathy, empathy, antipathy, pathos, pathetic, sociopath, passion, compassion, impassive, pathology**

ASSUAGE v. *to ease or relieve something that hurts or is worrisome; to quiet, pacify; to appease*
So that's my Parent-Management Tip of the Week, I guess: The best way to *assuage* your folks' worries is to tell them what really happened. *Assuaging* someone's fears isn't always this easy, of course, because sometimes truth is painful.

MEMORY FIX
Write each of these new words now, along with a synonym or definition for each. It helps to say them aloud as you write.

FIND THE SYNONYMS Answers on page 251

> **From the word choices offered below, select the missing synonym for each numbered word group.**

amiable   benign   amity   apathetic   dispassionate
jocular   elated   serene   frivolity   effervescent

1 joyous silliness   costly trifle   unseemly humor
_____

2 pleasant   easygoing   friendly   amicable
_____

3 high-spirited   overjoyed   filled with pleasure
_____

4 emotionless   unaffected by feelings _____

5 revealing no emotion   impassive _____

6 bubbling with enthusiasm   exhilarated
_____

7 placid   calm   quiet   peaceful   unflappable
_____

8 benevolent   kind   favorable   gentle
_____

9 friendship   accord   harmonious relations
_____

10 jocose   lighthearted   humorous   jocund
_____

141

FILL IN THE BLANKS

Answers on page 251

> Select the new word in List 18 that best
> completes the meaning and logic of each phrase.
> Remember to use the correct form of the word.

1 benefited from the _____ influence of the monks

2 a travelogue that _____ the many virtues of Spain

3 a nature so serene, so eternally _____ , that I wondered if she had any passion at all

4 with more _____ than a bottle of soda pop

5 a serious attempt to _____ the deteriorating state of the building

6 a(n) _____ but enjoyable way to blow all of my allowance

7 amusing Noel Coward play, _____ *Spirit*, about a humorous, cheerful ghost

8 thoughtful talk that attempted to _____ our fears about the upcoming changes

9 announcing his promotion with obvious _____

10 a(n) _____ note meant to _____ Grandma after we'd made a mess in her yard

FIND THE ANTONYMS   Answers on page 251

> **Match up the opposites by writing them on the correct lines.**

_____	**1.** elated	dispassionate
_____	**2.** impassive	censure
_____	**3.** appease	overwrought
_____	**4.** passionate	downcast
_____	**5.** extol	irritate
_____	**6.** sensible	effervescent
_____	**7.** placid	frivolous

MIGHTY OBVIOUS OPPOSITES

---

partial/impartial • potent/impotent • inflate/deflate • famous/infamous • savory/unsavory • tangible/intangible • auspicious/inauspicious • discriminate/ indiscriminate • consent/dissent • neutral/ biased

---

PARTIAL adj. *biased or even strongly disposed toward; or, referring to a portion of a whole*
IMPARTIAL adj. *unbiased, not prejudiced; fair, evenhanded*
At election time, journalists need to be *impartial* in their coverage of all candidates. Even if they're *partial* to one, they should avoid showing that *partiality* in print.

POTENT adj. *strong, powerful; effective (as "a potent remedy")*
IMPOTENT adj. *lacking effectiveness; weak, lacking strength*
Age proves to us that words are *potent* weapons. As kids we chanted, "Sticks and stones may break my bones, but words will never harm me." Yet we knew way back then that words were far from *impotent*.

INFLATE v. *to blow or puff up, either literally or figuratively; to expand or enlarge, sometimes unwisely*
DEFLATE v. *to let the air out of, thereby reducing in size, either a tire or someone's ego*
As we *inflated* balloons to celebrate Greg's victory as class president, I could see his ego *inflating*, too. "Hey, buddy," I said, to *deflate* him a bit before he got too obnoxious, "there's a zit on your nose."

CRAC/CRAT = to rule

autocrat—*one who makes and executes the laws; dictator*
> iron rule of the *autocrat*
> a clearly *autocratic* decision

aristocracy—*a privileged class; certain well-qualified people; an upper class of hereditary nobility*
> the local *aristocracy*
> fine, *aristocratic* bearing

Also: **democrat, democracy, theocracy, plutocracy, aristocrat**

FAMOUS adj. *widely known; outstanding, noted, excellent* adv. **famously,** *very or extremely*

INFAMOUS adj. *of exceedingly bad repute; disgraceful* n. **infamy**

Our family has a set of widely diverse twins, one *famous* for his generosity, the other *infamous* for deceiving everyone he meets. That kind of *infamy* I can live without!

SAVORY adj. *very tasty, palatable; referring to a good reputation; edifying or mind-pleasing*

UNSAVORY adj. *smelling or tasting bad; morally repugnant or disgusting; distasteful*

In merrie olde England, a meat *savory* was a spiced meat dish served as an appetizer. Now, because the word's meaning has grown, you can be a person with a *savory* reputation (excellent) who enjoys *savory* foods (tasty) while writing a collection of *savory* essays (mind-pleasing). Of course, anything *unsavory* is highly suspect, like that fellow who has an *unsavory* reputation.

TANGIBLE adj. *real, concrete, able to be touched (palpable); perceptible*

INTANGIBLE adj. *not concrete; impalpable yet real, such as cheerfulness*

Labeled a "decade of greed," the 1980s were a time when people eagerly acquired impressive *tangible* property, such as luxury cars and huge houses. Perhaps the new century will see an emphasis on *intangible* assets, like concern for others.

DEM = people

demagogue—*false leader who tells people what they want to hear, using popular prejudices to win approval*

     the latest *demagogue* in office

     empty talk of a *demagogue*

pandemic—*throughout an entire* (**pan**) *population* (**dem**)

     pandemic illness

     a tendency to become *pandemic*

Also: **epidemic, democrat, democracy, endemic, demographics**

AUSPICIOUS adj. *highly favorable; propitious* n. **auspice,** *a prophetic sign*

INAUSPICIOUS adj. *unfavorable; foreboding ill*
The Roman *auspex* divined the future by studying the flight and feeding patterns of birds. If the *auspices* were *auspicious*, he advised a ruler to act confidently. *Inauspicious* signs foretold trouble. When my car's engine overheated, I knew that was a very *inauspicious* sign.

DISCRIMINATE v. *to notice differences, distinguish clearly between objects or choices; to treat differently*

INDISCRIMINATE adj. *at random, without discrimination; haphazard*
I can easily *discriminate* among various pizzas and tell you which is best and why. I would never grab any old piece of pizza, making a totally *indiscriminate* choice, because pizza is important to me.

CONSENT n. *agreement; acceptance* v. **consent,** *to agree to*

DISSENT n. *disagreement* v. **dissent,** *to disagree*
Class presidents obtained the *consent* of each class before a large donated sum was spent on band uniforms and equipment. Of course, some sports fans *dissented*, but they were overruled for once.

NEUTRAL adj. *without bias or prejudice; neither for nor against*

BIASED adj. *prejudiced; having a distinct feeling one way or another*
Modern Sweden is a *neutral* country that has not taken sides in a war or funded a "war chest" like the United States. The United States, *biased* in favor of

democracy, has spent billions promoting that method of government and defending it.

MEMORY FIX

This time, write down only the words you DO NOT KNOW and their meanings. Say these words aloud as you write them.

WORDS IN CONTEXT   Answers on page 251

> **Write the meaning of each *italicized* word on the line provided.**

1 the most *unsavory* concoction I ever saw

_____

2 an *inflated* idea of his own importance

_____

3 the immensity of the problem made her feel totally *impotent*

_____

4 always *partial* to something chocolate

_____

5 the *intangible* reward of their gratitude

_____

6 his A+ was an *auspicious* beginning for the year

_____

7 giving out candy with an *indiscriminate* hand

_____

8 Clay's ability to turn *dissent* into compromise

9 choose consensus rather than the dictates of an *autocrat*

_____

10 a member of the feline *aristocracy*, unlike our Meatloaf

_____

TRUE OR FALSE Answers on page 251

> Read each sentence to see how the words in List 19 are being used. Then mark T (true) or F (false) beside each.

1 A *demagogue* uses both candor and sincerity.

_____

2 One reason to select jurors with care is to eliminate *biased* individuals and choose *impartial* ones. _____

3 Vampires scoff at *potent* spells against them.

_____

4 Fans hang around stage doors hoping for a glimpse of the most *infamous* stars. _____

5 I'd be eager to taste a *savory* dish offered as *tangible* proof of your culinary skills. _____

6 Mozart's talent was so great that it is sometimes difficult to *discriminate* between early works and later ones. _____

7 The various cold viruses are properly termed *pandemic*. _____

8 Blue skies are an *inauspicious* omen in the morning. _____

9 *Deflated* team spirits can translate into a quick loss of yardage on the football field. _____

10 The more you know about a subject, the harder it may be to remain totally *neutral*. _____

LIST 20 COMPLIMENT? NOT!

didactic • fickle • gullible • insipid • petty • incorrigible • officious • pompous • inane • willful • tedious • wanton

---

DIDACTIC adj. *instructive, designed to teach; morally "preachy"; pedantic*
The word *didactic* originated in Greece and meant "apt in teaching." Today, anything described as *didactic* is apt to be preachy, dull, or both.

FICKLE adj. *changeable, inconstant, irresolute; not steadfast*
The faithless behavior of a *fickle* lover is the subject of the old country-western favorite, "Your Cheatin' Heart." One sex is always accusing the other of being *fickle*.

GULLIBLE adj. *easily fooled; naive, ingenuous, innocent*
A *gullible* person swallows whatever you tell him, maybe down his gullet? And a *gull* is a fool or dupe who's easily decieved. Remember that *gullible* fellow who thought he was buying the Brooklyn Bridge for $24?

INSIPID adj. *lacking flavor, zip, or interest; dull, flat*
To French novelist Anatole France, "A tale without love is like beef without mustard: *insipid*." (What a thoroughly French analogy.) *Mais oui*, the world would be an infinitely more *insipid* place without love and mustard.

PETTY adj. *of minor importance; small-minded*
Near the end of *Macbeth*, King Macbeth says, "Tomorrow, and tomorrow, and tomorrow/Creeps in this *petty* pace from day to day," beginning a world-famous soliloquy. In modern use, anything *petty* is usually small-minded in nature.

> **DOG/DOX = opinion, praise**
>
> **dogmatic**—*stubbornly opinionated; dictatorial; doctrinaire*
>
> > the autocrat's *dogmatic* approach
> > unpopular *dogmatic* style
>
> **orthodox**—*according to traditional teaching or established religious doctrine; "by the book"*
>
> > in an *orthodox* manner
> > comfortable, *orthodox* presentation
>
> Also: **dogma, doxology, paradox, heterodox**

INCORRIGIBLE adj. *extremely difficult to manage or control; delinquent, recalcitrant*
Having lived with two *incorrigible* pets, I understand this word. Our own *incorrigible* cat sleeps in the clothes dryer but doesn't enjoy tumbling about on high heat.

OFFICIOUS adj. *self-important and meddlesome; interfering; impertinent*
An *officious* person is a "buttinski"; you know the type. As writer Ivan Krylov put it, "Heaven save you from a foolish friend; the too *officious* fool is worse than any foe."

POMPOUS adj. *puffed up with self-importance; arrogant*
Just as unpopular as the "officious fool" is the "*pompous* fool"—someone dying to impress you with his importance or knowledge. Unfortunately, one afflicted with *pomposity* is all too often known for verbosity as well.

INANE adj. *witless, empty, insipid, "dopey"*
The best *inane* giggle in show business belonged to Butterfly McQueen, who played the part of a witless young girl in *Gone With the Wind*. Only a fine actress like Ms. McQueen could have created such a believably *inane* yet lovable character.

WILLFUL adj. *headstrong; stubbornly self-willed; unruly*
Incorrigible pets like ours are *willful* ones, determined to do what they want just like young children. Once when Eddie didn't get his way, he ground a banana

into our new rug, a *willful* act that got him into a lot of trouble.

TEDIOUS adj. *tiresome, boring; seeming too long or dull*

Anatole France, a most quotable satirist, wrote that "historical books which contain no lies are extremely *tedious*." History is fascinating if you like it, of course, and only *tedious* if you don't.

DOC/DACT = to teach

docile—*easily controlled or taught; compliant, tractable, amenable, obedient*
    a *docile* breed of cows
    a sweet, *docile* child

indoctrinate—*to teach the basics; teach a specific point of view*
    indoctrinated by church leaders
    indoctrinate new members

Also: **doctor, doctrine, doctrinaire, didactic**

WANTON adj. *arousing sexual desire; lacking human kindness (as in "wanton cruelty"); malicious; unchecked (as in "a wanton growth of weeds")*

Behind all the meanings of *wanton* is the idea of uncontrolled behavior. Not all things need control, of course, such as wildflowers that grow on the hillsides in *wanton* profusion.

MEMORY FIX

As with the last list, write down only the words you don't know or are unsure about. As you note their meanings, say each word aloud.

SUBSTITUTION Answers on page 251

Replace each *italicized* word or phrase with the
correct new word from List 20.

1 The salesman delivered a *teaching* talk that was
surprisingly interesting and convincing.

_____

2 "I guess I'm sort of *easily deceived*," my cousin
Sara confessed later, hiding her latest purchase
behind her back. _____

3 "Maybe I'm even *impossible to control*," she
went on miserably, "because I always fall for a
good spiel."

_____

4 I shrugged and gave her an *empty, silly* smile, but
her *loose and uncontrolled* purchases were
getting on my nerves. _____ _____

5 "Well," I harrumphed, "I don't mean to be
tiresome or boring, but shouldn't you quit this?"

_____

6 Sara gave me a smile that was anything but
obedient and said, "You don't need to act so
self-important!" _____ _____

7 I mumbled, "Sorry. I hate people who are
meddlesome and interfering." _____

8 "That's better," she replied. "It's not like you to
be *small-minded*, either, so let's forget it."

_____

153

9 "Sure. Just put that food grinder away with all the others," I said, not caring that I sounded *dictatorial*. _____

10 Defeated, she gave me a(n) *zestless* smile. "Ah, clever cousin. How did you know it was another food grinder?" _____

MATCHING Answers on page 251

From the list below, find two synonyms for each numbered word and write them in on the correct lines.

pedantic	unchecked	naive	established	delinquent
inconstant	flavorless	preachy	tractable	ingenuous
witless	recalcitrant	insipid	traditional	inhumane
compliant	changeable	dull	interfering	impertinent

1 fickle _____ _____

2 gullible _____ _____

3 insipid _____ _____

4 didactic _____ _____

5 incorrigible _____ _____

6 inane _____ _____

7 wanton _____ _____

8 orthodox _____ _____

9 docile _____ _____

10 officious _____ _____

FIND THE ODDBALL   Answers on page 251

> In each word group, cross out the oddball—the
> one unrelated word or phrase.

1 mean-spirited   ugly   unimportant   minor   petty

2 unsavory   self-important   arrogant   pompous
puffed-up

3 unruly   willful   stubbornly determined
headstrong   biased

4 theoretical   traditional   orthodox   established

5 instruct   train   indoctrinate   teach a
doctrine   moderate

6 fickle   doctrinaire   dogmatic   opinionated
dictatorial

155

REVIEW: LISTS 16–20

Just in case a few words from lists 16–20 have gone astray, it's time to review. Read those lists again, then you can whip through these few reminder-type exercises.

ANALOGIES Answers on page 241

Choose the one word pair in each list below that expresses the same relationship as the pair in capital letters.

1 REASONING : FALLACIOUS

(A) logic : dispassionate
(B) behavior : docile
(C) ruling : orthodox
(D) judgment : biased
(E) demeanor : amiable

2 INFAMY : CENSURE

(A) studies : indoctrinate
(B) pettiness : extricate
(C) virtue : extol
(D) amity : savor
(E) novelty : enjoin

3 PLEASANT : JOCULAR

(A) insipid : inane
(B) famous : cultured
(C) serene : placid
(D) clement : mild
(E) contented : blithe

4 DEMAGOGUE : SINCERITY

(A) neophyte : experience
(B) feline : indolence
(C) aristocracy : dogma
(D) conflict : jeopardy
(E) autocrat : pomposity

5 EFFERVESCENT : ELATION

    (A) overjoyed : emulation
    (B) deflated : repudiation
    (C) incorrigible : apathy
    (D) indecision : clemency
    (E) impassive : discrimination

6 CONFIDENCE : UNDERMINE

    (A) capital : squander
    (B) fears : assuage
    (C) donation : solicit
    (D) consent : extort
    (E) embankment : erode

MATCHING ANTONYMS   Answers on page 252

> **Match the antonyms by writing the correct opposite beside each numbered word.**

_____ **1.** intangible   ominous, foreboding

_____ **2.** officious   similarity

_____ **3.** wanton   ineffective

_____ **4.** expedite   agreement

_____ **5.** ameliorate   engrossing, absorbing

_____ **6.** auspicious   disgrace

_____ **7.** dissent   implicate

_____ **8.** tedious   concrete

_____ **9.** potent   aggravate

_____ **10.** esteem   humble

_____ **11.** disparity   carefully controlled

_____ **12.** extricate   hinder

FIND THOSE SYNONYMS

Answers on page 252

> On the lines provided, write the two best synonyms from this list of words to complete each numbered word group.

repeal	enjoin	unfeeling	impede	assuage
vacillating	hinder	inconstant	amicable	insipid
conciliate	novice	call back	crooked	empty
command	tortuous	gregarious	beginner	apathetic

1 hamper _____ obstruct _____

2 rescind _____ annul _____

3 _____ forbid _____ prohibit

4 _____ twisted _____ winding

5 fledgling _____ tyro _____

6 sociable _____ convivial _____

7 _____ fickle _____ changeable

8 _____ appease _____ pacify

9 impassive _____ indifferent _____

10 inane _____ silly _____

GOOD WORDS GET AROUND

Answers on page 252

> **From the words listed below, fill in the blanks in these quotations.**

alleviates   squander   petty   placid
frivolous   dogmatic   undermining   impartial

1 "To waste, to destroy our natural resources, to skin and exhaust the land instead of using it so as to increase its usefulness, will result in _____ in the days of our children the very prosperity which we ought by right to hand down to them amplified and developed."

—Theodore Roosevelt, address to Congress, 1907

2 "Pale Death with _____ tread beats at the poor man's cottage door and at the palace of kings."

—Horace, Roman poet and satirist

3 "Dost thou love life? Then do not _____ time; for that's the stuff life is made of."

—Benjamin Franklin, *Poor Richard's Almanack*

4 "There is a strange charm in the thoughts of a good legacy . . . which wondrously _____ the sorrow that men would otherwise feel for the death of friends."

—Miguel Cervantes, *Don Quixote*

159

5 "I think I could turn and live with animals, they are so _____ and self-contained."

—Walt Whitman, *Song of Myself*

6 "One who is serious all day will never have a good time, while one who is _____ all day will never establish a household."

—Ancient Egyptian maxim

7 "When people are least sure, they are often most _____ ." (Look for irony here.)

—John Kenneth Galbraith, American economist

8 "Why, man, he [Caesar] doth bestride the narrow world

Like a Colossus; and we _____ men

Walk under his huge legs, and peep about

To find ourselves dishonourable graves."

—Shakespeare, *Julius Caesar*

LIST 21 — AH, THE PRUDENT PURITANS

frugal • exemplary • diligent • prudent • scrupulous • parochial • pious • discreet • thrifty • solemn • pragmatic • steadfast

FRUGAL adj. *careful in using resources; sparing, thrifty*
Since I got my car, which eats cash, I've had to be *frugal* in all my spending. I can't keep this money-guzzler going unless *frugality* is my motto from now on.

EXEMPLARY adj. *serving as a model; commendable*
I had an *exemplary* month recently—didn't buy any extras—but did the car reward me with *exemplary* behavior? Hardly. It blew its head gasket.

DILIGENT adj. *showing painstaking care and attention*
I'll have to slave *diligently* for months to pay off this repair, and I bet it was my fault. The engine overheated because I wasn't *diligent* about keeping the radiator full.

PRUDENT adj. *shrewd and careful in managing things; wise; discreet, circumspect; also, frugal*
Luckily I know a *prudent* auto mechanic, Raoul, who owns a small local garage. Raoul hires only the best repairmen and *prudently* stocks rebuilt parts as well.

SCRUPULOUS adj. *showing painstaking care; extremely attentive to detail or to morality*
"A real mechanic," says Raoul, "pays *scrupulous* attention to details. I examine every connection, every hose, *scrupulously*, because overlooking even one thing can be disastrous."

PAROCHIAL adj. *of narrow, limited scope; provincial; referring to a church parish*

GEN = kind, race, birth, cause

congenial—*having kindred tastes; like-minded; sociable*

> a pleasant, *congenial* fellow
> having a *congenial* outlook

generic—*universal, general; referring to a group or class*

> a bottle of *generic* aspirin
> a *generic* form of gelatin

Also: **ingenuous** *(naive)*, **engender** *(foster, begin)*, **gentleman, disingenuous** *(faking honesty)*, **homogeneous** (The **gen** words love to appear on SATs.)

In addition to his ownership of the garage, Raoul has a *parochial* job as a lay priest. Until I got to know him, I had a totally uninformed and *parochial* view of his religion.

PIOUS adj. *noticeably religious, sometimes to the point of hypocrisy; or, honestly religious and devoted* n. **piety**

Even if he is a lay priest, Raoul doesn't go around making *pious* comments about religion all the time. His *piety* is real, not phony; anyone can tell how sincere he is.

DISCREET adj. *showing good sense (prudence) in behavior; circumspect; modest (as in "discreet of speech")* n. **discretion**

Dad and I had one of those *discreet*, father-son talks last night, away from the rest of the family. Of course,

CRED = to believe

credible—*believable, trustworthy; worthy of being believed*

> a *credible* witness
> would never question his *credibility*

credulous—*willing to believe almost anything; gullible*

> a young, *credulous* person
> a *credulous* dog, easily fooled

Also: **incredible** *(amazing)*, **incredulous** *(unbelieving)*, **credit, creditable, discredit, credentials**

any kid should use some *discretion* when he's talking to a parent, but Dad and I have always been pretty open with each other.

THRIFTY adj. *extremely careful with money; provident, sparing, frugal* n. **thrift**
"You'll have to be extra *thrifty*," Dad said, "to pay off a repair bill that size. I've always been a rather *thrifty* fellow myself, so I can afford to lend you money at no interest—how's that?"

SOLEMN adj. *extremely serious; sober, sedate*
I'd already worked out a payment schedule with Raoul, so I made Dad a *solemn* promise that he didn't have to worry about me and my car. "I admire the way you're handling this, Ted," Dad said, pretty *solemn* himself.

PRAGMATIC adj. *practical, not idealistic; sensible* n. **pragmatist** *(person) and* **pragmatism**

I thought I'd made a normal, *pragmatic* arrangement to pay my bill, so I was surprised by Dad's praise. Now that I own a car that eats money, I'm forced to operate in a more *pragmatic*, thoughtful way.

STEADFAST adj. *not apt to change; steady, faithful, loyal*
My friend Greg really fits the word *steadfast*, even if it sounds old-fashioned. In fact, he's such a *steadfast* friend that he's paying part of my repair bill, because he always depends on me for his transportation.

MEMORY FIX
On a separate piece of paper, just like before, write down each word in this list along with a definition and say each one aloud.

163

FILL IN THE BLANKS

Answers on page 252

> **Select the new word from List 21 that best completes the meaning and logic of each sentence. Alter the form of the word as needed for sense.**

1 She's so _____ she'd believe anything you tell her.

2 Jana needs to give _____ attention to that experiment so that each chemical is added at the right time.

3 _____ is a perfect antonym of fickle.

4 The prodigal spender is the antithesis of the _____ soul who lives a life based on _____ .

5 A crazy idealist like Don Quixote is clearly not a _____ .

6 Little Lord Fauntleroy and Miss Goody Two-Shoes were known for their _____ conduct.

7 Turn six words from this lesson into nouns, and you have six virtues esteemed by the Puritans: _____ , _____ , _____ , _____ , _____ , and _____ .

8 The Puritanical outlook was unfortunately _____ , an irony when you consider that they settled the colonies to escape prejudice.

9 The Puritans are always portrayed as a somber lot, known for their _____ of manner and clothing to match.

10 It took only a brief time to establish the _____ of _____ drugs, which are the same as the name brands but without the big price tag.

ADD THE SYNONYMS Answers on page 252

> **From List 21's word list, definitions, and synonyms, complete each numbered word group.**

1 thrifty _____ prudent _____

2 circumspect _____ discreet

3 of a church parish _____ provincial

4 praiseworthy commendable _____ acting as a model

5 attentive to detail _____ showing painstaking care

6 loyal _____ steady _____

7 like-minded _____ sociable _____

TRUE OR FALSE Answers on page 252

> **Read the sentences below and then mark T (true) or F (false) for each.**

1 The most effective liar is a wholly *credible* one. _____

2 You might as well dismiss an accountant who's been accused of *scrupulousness*. _____

165

3 The name THRIFT DRUG encourages you to think it will be a *prudent* place to shop. _____

4 Puritans would have preferred a little levity or frivolity in church compared to all that *solemnity* they endured. _____

5 Say that a president is a *pragmatist* and he's doomed. _____

6 The older you get, the more *credulous* you're apt to be. _____

7 Because *generic* products don't pay for advertising, they can be sold at lower costs. _____

8 The best college roommate would be a *congenial* person. _____

LIST 22 OUT OF THIS WORLD

clairvoyant • chimera • eccentric • karma • enigma • vicarious • hypothetical • cryptic • esoteric • oblivious • utopia • elusive

CLAIRVOYANT n. *one who perceives far more than the normal five senses would explain; a seer* adj. *extraordinarily perceptive* n. **clairvoyance**

In the days before science took hold, people turned to a *clairvoyant* for explanations of the inexplicable. In the twentieth century, only those who study paranormal psychology are comfortable with the possibility of true *clairvoyance* in humans.

CHIMERA n. *a Greek mythic being with a lion's head, goat's body, and a serpent's tail* adj. **chimerical,** *fanciful, imaginary, improbable, foolish*

"What a *chimera* then is man! What a novelty! . . . the glory and the shame of the universe," said Blaise Pascal, a seventeenth-century French mathematician and philosopher. For centuries, philosophers have debated the *chimerical* nature of humankind.

ECCENTRIC adj. *decidedly odd or unusual; aberrational* n. *an odd person* pl. **eccentricities, oddities, aberrations**

Always try for the part of an *eccentric* in a play, because a quirky character is easier to portray and usually steals the show. Remember the hilarious *eccentricities* of Oscar and Felix in *The Odd Couple*?

KARMA n. *your life force that determines your fate or destiny in the next life (Hinduism, Buddhism)*

What is *karma* for the Buddhist is *kismet* for the Arab or Turk. "You must mean predestination," says the Presbyterian. Whether we call it *karma* or something else, everyone would like to explain why life unfolds as it does.

ENIGMA n. *a riddle hard to puzzle out; conundrum; mystery*

Early in World War II, Churchill broadcast to his English audience: "I cannot forecast to you the action of Russia. It is a riddle wrapped in a mystery inside an *enigma*." And for the modern generation, Russia still appears *enigmatic*.

VICARIOUS adj. *felt or experienced secondhand, through someone else or through another medium*

Riding a roller coaster is a real thrill, not a *vicarious* experience. Anyone wanting *vicarious* terror can go to the movies or turn on the TV.

HYPOTHETICAL adj. *based on a hypothesis (a logical theory) rather than on reality; conjectural*

Most of our accepted scientific laws began as a logical conjecture, a *hypothetical* "What if . . ." that led to experiments that proved the initial *hypothesis*.

CRYPTIC adj. *obscure; intentionally mysterious*

My buddies from Y camp recalled a *cryptic* code we invented one summer. Every summer after that we sent each other *cryptic* messages, especially when we were planning a trip across the lake to the girls' camp.

ESOTERIC adj. *of knowledge belonging to initiated people*

Twins often develop an *esoteric* language that no one else understands. When I listen to Dad and some of his chemist friends talking, I know that advanced chemistry has its own *esoteric* vocabulary, too.

OBLIVIOUS n. *totally unaware (usu. with "of" or "to")*

Mom accuses us kids of being *oblivious* to dirt and mess. It's not that we're *oblivious* exactly, it's just that we're more skilled at ignoring that stuff than most adults.

CHRON = time

anachronism—*a thing out of place in time*
　　an *anachronism* like the steam engine or a
　　peddler's cart
chronic—*habitual, repetitive, long-lasting, frequent*
　　a *chronic* worrywart
　　seems to have a *chronic* cold
Also: **chronology, synchronize, chronological, chronicle**

UTOPIA n. *a place where everything about life is perfect*
Meaning "nowhere" in Greek, *utopia* is a place so perfect that it's a pity it exists only in an old novel.

(Dystopia was the place where everything was as bad as possible.) A great deal of literature centers on *utopian* longings for an ideal world.

ELUSIVE adj. *apt to evade pursuit or definition (as "an elusive thought"); hard to pin down, identify* v. **elude**

> "We seek him here, we seek him there,
> Those Frenchies seek him everywhere.
> Is he in heaven?—Is he in hell?
> That demmed, *elusive* Pimpernel?"

Throughout this swashbuckling novel by Orczy, the Scarlet Pimpernel made it his business to *elude* his captors.

MEMORY FIX
As before, write down each word you don't know, with definitions for each, and say them all aloud.

169

SUBSTITUTION Answers on page 253

> Replace each *italicized* word or phrase with the
> correct word from List 22's word and root lists.
> Change the word's form if necessary for
> grammatical correctness.

1 dispute could last forever unless you *come in between* _____

2 a wounded man, *unaware* of the fight continuing around him _____

3 gave me a(n) *mysterious* glance I couldn't interpret _____

4 not an actual project yet, purely *based on conjecture* _____

5 a *fantastic* plan that had no prayer of being successful _____

6 lost language of the Druids, along with all their *known only to certain people* lore _____

7 don't know whether it was dumb luck or simply my *destiny* _____

8 the *hard to track* fragrance of an elegant perfume _____

9 *extremely odd* behavior that is without *an antecedent* _____ _____

10 a(n) *frequent* yearning for *a perfect place* _____ _____

TRUE OR FALSE   Answers on page 253

> Read each sentence to see how the words in
> List 22 are being used. Then mark T (true) or F
> (false) beside each one.

1 Shakespeare's reference to a clock on the wall in
Julius Caesar is an example of an *anachronism*
in literature. _____

2 Cassandra the *Clairvoyant* would be a good name
for the Trojan woman who said, "Beware of
Greeks bearing gifts." _____

3 The influence of gravity remains a *hypothetical*
topic, still under discussion at Dr. Newton's
house. _____

4 It hardly requires any *esoteric* information to
interpret the Dead Sea scrolls. _____

5 If you're reading a book and fall downstairs,
blame it on your bad *karma*, not just inattention.
_____

6 Nothing is easier to unravel than a classic
enigma. _____

7 If I allude to your successful stickup at the bank
around my police sergeant uncle, you'd better get
ready to *elude* his pursuit. _____

171

MATCHING

Answers on page 253

> Circle the two words or phrases that best explain the meaning of each word in bold type.

1 **unprecedented**   illegal   without example   annoying   novel

2 **clairvoyant**   weird   perceptive   a seer   persnickety

3 **eccentric**   unacceptable   fruity   aberrational   odd

4 **cryptic**   undecipherable   enigmatic   deadly   referring to burial

5 **oblivious**   "out to lunch"   clueless   confused   panicky

6 **intercede**   debate   intervene   dispute   mediate

7 **chronic**   repetitive   infectious   long-lasting   tardy

8 **vicarious**   exciting   lively   secondhand   substitutionary

9 **utopian**   ideal   unreal   perfect   impossible

10 **chimerical**   frightening   fanciful   miraculous   imaginary

172

BIG, FAT, GLORIOUS ADJECTIVES

virulent • whimsical • voluminous • ubiquitous • turbulent • haphazard • precocious • vindictive • unimpeachable • voracious • homogeneous • incongruous

VIRULENT adj. *full of malignant or evil intent; noted for fast, powerful, often fatal progress*
Tuberculosis, always a *virulent* disease, keeps coming back for another round. Though streptomycin cured the old strains, new and more *virulent* ones require new medication.

WHIMSICAL adj. *based on a whim or fancy; capricious*

Sometimes a *whimsical* longing for the ocean comes over me, and a bunch of us pile in the car and head out, even in winter. The occasional *whimsical* idea makes life more fun.

VOLUMINOUS adj. *extremely large in volume or size; also, numerous (as in "voluminous notes")*
You don't see *voluminous* skirts anymore, except on some wedding dresses. The only *voluminous* thing in my life right now is the pile of notes for my history paper on the Supreme Court.

UBIQUITOUS adj. *seemingly everywhere; widespread*
MacDonald's restaurants, *ubiquitous* today, were scarce just thirty years ago. Now the chain has flung its *ubiquitous* Golden Arches over all of Europe, even Russia.

TURBULENT adj. *marked by roiling, turmoil, and unrest; seething, agitated*

```
ANIMA = mind, soul, spirit
```
animosity—*hatred, antagonism, ill will, enmity*

>an *animosity* that went back in time
>unjustified *animosity*

equanimity—*coolness or evenness of disposition; balance*

>admired the *equanimity* that never deserted him

Also: **animal, animus, animated, unanimous, magnanimous, pusillanimous** *(cowardly)*

The last half of our senior year is a *turbulent* time when so much is going on. This *turbulence* fills our minds, too, so that finding ways to relax is critical.

HAPHAZARD adj. *unplanned; happening by chance, at random; aimless* (**hap** = *luck or chance*)
The "hap" words are strewn *haphazardly* throughout the English language. Consider, for example, *happen, happenstance, mayhap, mishap, happy-go-lucky*, and *perhaps*. Originally, *happy* meant "lucky." It's not just a *haphazard* connection, either; of course you'd be happy if you were lucky.

PRECOCIOUS adj. *showing very early mental development (L. = "precooked" or "prematurely ripe")*
Everyone hates baby-sitting a kid whose parent brags, "Oh, he's always been *precocious*." The early mastery of language and logic by the *precocious* child is a lousy excuse for rude behavior.

VINDICTIVE adj. *eager for revenge; spiteful*
A *vindictive* spirit keeps a fight going, such as the famous Hatfield-McCoy feud in Appalachia. And isn't there something awfully *vindictive* about the ancient code of Hammurabi, which read, "An eye for an eye; a tooth for a tooth"?

UNIMPEACHABLE adj. *blameless, irreproachable; not open to accusation*
For my history paper, I went to an *unimpeachable* source of Supreme Court information: a sitting Justice. If a Justice's honor isn't absolutely *unimpeachable*, then no one's is.

VORACIOUS adj. *insatiably hungry for something; ravenous*

> **VI/VIT/VIV = life**
>
> **viable**—*capable of living; able to work or develop acceptably or even well*
>> a *viable* fetus
>> a *viable* product
>> a *viable* candidate
>
> **convivial**—*friendly and lively of spirit, party-loving*
>> a noisy, *convivial* gathering
>> her open, *convivial* nature
>
> Also: **vital, vitamin, revitalize, vitality, vivid, revive, vivisection, vivacity, vivacious**

Kids who "tear up" the SATs and PSATs are the ones who've always been *voracious* readers. Greg's been a *voracious* eater for the last six years; now he's working on the reading.

HOMOGENEOUS adj. *being the same or alike throughout (lit. "the same kind"); also,* **homogenous**

Countries such as Sweden and Denmark tend to be extremely *homogeneous*, while the United States is less *homogenized* every day as the unhappy from afar find refuge here. Diversity of people makes life more interesting, but it is also more challenging than *homogeneity*.

INCONGRUOUS adj. *seeming out of place or unsuited*

A tuxedo would look totally *incongruous* in our school, except on Live Character Day. That day, we all dressed as our favorite literary character, and nothing seemed *incongruous*, especially not the terrific pig costume I wore as Wilbur.

MEMORY FIX

You know the routine. Write down each word you don't know, along with its definition, and say each word aloud.

175

FILL-IN CHART Answers on page 253

Fill in the missing boxes with information learned in List 23.

WORD	PREFIX/ROOT	TWO SYNONYMS/ DEFINITION
1.	**dic/dict** = say	revengeful,
2. turbulent	**turb** = agitate	
3.	**homo** = same **gen** = kind	same or alike throughout
4.	**anim** = spirit, soul	enmity,
5.	**hap** = luck, chance	
6.	**equ** = equal, same **anim** = spirit, soul	
7. virulent	**virus** = poison	
8. convivial	**con** = with; **viv** = life	
9.	**ubique** = everywhere	everywhere,
10. precocious	**pre** = before **coquere** = cooked	

RHYME TIME Answers on page 253

Complete these lines of admittedly awful poetry with words from List 23.

1 In the narrow coal shaft, hunting bituminous
Forswear all garments considered _____ .

2 Vicki suffered for hours from insects
_____ ,
She dug at the bites and swore, Goodness
Gracious!
Smearing her body with calamine lotion
Was more than just a _____ notion.

3 It's an overused buzzword; I refuse to be liable,
That tired, _____ adjective
_____ .

4 Our purebred came with papers _____ ,
Sad to say, he has proved unteachable.

5 Students teaching classes is not an _____
thought,
We remember well what our peers have taught.

WORD ANALYSIS Answers on page 253

Fill in the most logical word for each sentence,
choosing from among the words presented in
List 23.

1 The child who is reading at age three is usually
described as _____ .

2 In the middle of a memorial service, giddy
laughter would seem not only _____ , but
also irreverent.

3 Thomas á Becket, who did not accede to all of
Henry II's wishes, was murdered in Canterbury
Cathedral not long after Henry allegedly cried,
"Who will rid me of the **t** _____ priest?"

4 Elementary kids have a _____ appetite for
information about dinosaurs.

5 You can tell that comedian Robin Williams gives
in to _____ flights of fancy as they occur to
him, ad libbing with a brilliance given only to a
few.

6 Universally, people revere magnanimity and fear
those with a _____ streak.

paradigm • unscathed • iconoclast • kindle • elaborate • tacit • peripheral • deter • propensity • discord • precipitate • unethical

PARADIGM n. *something serving as a model or ideal*

For years, our class unknowingly acted as a *paradigm* for classes after us. We didn't plan to be a model class, but we gradually realized that we were the acknowledged *paradigm*.

UNSCATHED adj. *unharmed, uninjured, untouched* adj. **scathing,** *bitterly severe, caustic*

No class is perfect, and ours won't graduate *unscathed*. This spring, our most outspoken students delivered some *scathing* criticism of the school to local newspaper reporters.

ICONOCLAST n. *one who criticizes established ideas or traditions (Gr. = image destroyer)*

These talkative students were known *iconoclasts*, of course, who'd rebelled for various reasons all through school. But we understood their *iconoclastic* views from long association and had always respected their ideas.

KINDLE v. *to start burning; to spark interest or curiosity*

Nothing *kindles* the interest of the public like a hot newspaper story. Our classmates' best suggestions for school reform *kindled* a desire in several parents to begin discussions with the school administration.

ELABORATE v. *to spell out specifically, in detail* adj. *detailed or complex; carefully planned*

Those interested parents asked our reform-minded classmates to *elaborate* on their ideas. While some of their concepts were too *elaborate* to implement, many

---

SED/SESS/SID = to sit or be still

assiduous—*marked by careful, diligent attention; persistent*
> *assiduously* cleaning his fur
> giving it *assiduous* attention

insidious—*dangerous but appealing; slow but steady in effect; subtle; settling in unnoticed (as in "an insidious disease")*
> an *insidious* illness
> the *insidious* lure of gambling

Also: **sedentary, sediment, supersede, preside, subsidy, dissident, resident, session, obsession, sedate**

---

of their suggestions met with approval, even requests for further *elaboration*.

TACIT adj. *understood though not spoken; silent*
Students and parents arrived at a *tacit* agreement that the parents would advance these novel ideas. Everyone *tacitly* acknowledged that parents would receive more serious attention from school officials.

PERIPHERAL adj. *around the edge or periphery; auxiliary; of minor, not central, importance*
The parents' committee decided to deal with only a few central issues and to ignore the *peripheral* ones. Just as *peripheral* (side) vision is less critical than forward vision, some of the students' ideas were less important.

DETER v. *to hinder or prevent from acting; to inhibit, turn aside or discourage* n. **deterrent**
Nothing would *deter* my parents from joining this group of adults bent on change. I had hoped that my begging for noninvolvement would be a *deterrent*, but it wasn't.

PROPENSITY n. *strong natural leaning or preference*
Have you noticed how your parents have a *propensity* for getting involved when you wish they wouldn't? The natural *propensity* of ostriches is to stick their heads in the sand, hoping to go unnoticed, but parents sure aren't like that.

> ### TEND/TENS/TENT = to stretch
> **tenuous**—*slight and insubstantial; flimsy, weak*
> > only a *tenuous* grasp of the subject
> > new and *tenuous* idea
>
> **extenuating**—*mitigating; reducing in severity or importance*
> > an *extenuating* circumstance that explained her lateness
>
> Also: **tendency, extend, extension, portent, portentous, contend, contentious, tension, tense, pretense**

DISCORD n. *lack of agreement or harmony; strife, tension*

The night the parents met with the school officials was marked at first by *discord*. The seeds of this *discord* had been sown by the newspaper story, of course.

PRECIPITATE v. *to cause to begin in an abrupt manner* adj. *unwisely fast, impetuous, headlong*

Although the newspaper article *precipitated* the parents' involvement with school policy, no one at the meeting wanted to plunge *precipitately* into massive changes.

UNETHICAL adj. *lacking moral principles (ethics)*

Closed meetings of public boards are *unethical* in our state. The "Sunshine Laws" insist that the operations—and therefore the *ethics*—of ruling boards should be open to scrutiny by their employers, the taxpayers.

MEMORY FIX

Now's the time to write down each word from this list that you don't know, along with its definition. Say each word aloud too. Remember why you're doing this? WRITING FIXES WORDS IN MIND.

FILL IN THE BLANKS Answers on page 253

> From the new words in List 24, select the one that best completes the meaning and logic of each phrase. Be sure to use the right form of each word.

1 there'll be a reason, some _____ explanation

2 always questioned authority, a(n) _____ from birth

3 suspected of _____ behavior in office

4 hoping to _____ a creative fire to last all autumn

5 a real enigma that needs precise _____ (use the noun)

6 didn't actually say yes, but nodded in _____ approval

7 a(n) _____ weed that seemed to spread overnight

8 so weak now that she has but a(n) _____ hold on life

9 cannot do drugs and expect to escape _____

10 a cat's inherited _____ for hunting prey

MATCHING ANTONYMS

Answers on page 253

> **From the word list below, find an opposite for each numbered word and write it on the appropriate line.**

traditionalist   kindle   deter   discord   elaborate
precipitate   peripheral   careless   spoken   honorable

1 unethical _____

2 central, main _____

3 douse _____

4 simple _____

5 harmony _____

6 encourage _____

7 tacit _____

8 considered _____

9 assiduous _____

10 iconoclast _____

MATCHING

Answers on page 254

> **In the group of words at the right, find two synonyms or phrases to write beside each of the words to the left.**

1 scathing

_____ dangerously alluring

_____ flimsy

lack of harmony

2 propensity

_____ impetuous

_____ discourage

model

3 peripheral

_____ caustic

_____ strife

admired example

4 discord

_____ tendency

_____ persistent

headlong

5 tenuous

_____ most attentive

_____ inhibit

barely perceptible

6 deter

_____ auxiliary

_____ highly critical

subtle

7 insidious

_____ around the edge

_____ inclination

8 paradigm

_____

_____

9 precipitate

_____

_____

10 assiduous

_____

_____

183

arbitrary • blatant • capricious • desultory • extraneous • flagrant • devious • compatible • detrimental • susceptible • resigned • sporadic

ARBITRARY adj. *according to choice or impulse, rather than merit; in a tyrannical or despotic way*
I made an *arbitrary* decision to serve pizza at the class party. When there isn't a chance to consult a group or take a vote, I prefer to make an *arbitrary* choice and not worry about it.

BLATANT adj. *embarrassingly obvious, loud, or showy; brazen, tasteless*
Nobody likes to make a *blatant* error in public because it's embarrassing. Showing up in clothes that prove to be *blatantly* out of place, for instance, is pretty awkward.

CAPRICIOUS adj. *not steady, changing on a whim or "caprice"*
The stereotype of a female movie star is that of a *capricious* airhead. Actually, a good actress tries to be wholly professional and leaves *capricious* behavior to butterflies.

DESULTORY adj. *in a random, unplanned fashion; haphazard*
Last weekend we struck off into the woods on a long, *desultory* ramble that took us to a creek we'd never seen before. That's the fun of excursions done in a *desultory* way; you never know what you'll discover.

EXTRANEOUS adj. *extra, nonessential, irrelevant*
"No *extraneous* chitchat," said the guidance counselor as he blue-penciled my essay for a college application. "Make a careful outline, then don't add even one *extraneous* word!"

FLAGRANT adj. *highly noticeable in a negative way; glaring*

On occasion, my cat Meatloaf goes for a stroll on the kitchen counters in *flagrant* disobedience of house rules. Cats are known for following their own interests, of course, no matter how *flagrant* their behavior.

DEVIOUS adj. *indirect, roundabout; cunning or deceptive; remote (as "a devious path through the woods")*

I can follow a trail, no matter how *devious*, but not the twists and turns of a *devious* mind. Perhaps the most infamous *devious* thinker was Nicolo Machiavelli; anything termed Machiavellian is noted for its cunning or duplicity.

COMPATIBLE adj. *well-suited; adaptable; related, similar*

Dogs and cats are supposed to be *incompatible*, but families with pets know better. A cat and dog raised together may be not only *compatible* but also very attached to one another. (Remember *The Incredible Journey*?)

DETRIMENTAL adj. *definitely harmful; damaging; pernicious*

Spraying hedgerows and ditches to kill weeds proved sadly *detrimental* to game birds like pheasants who lost their nesting sites. Modern ecologists know that we must stop any practice that is a *detriment* to our nation's wildlife.

SUSCEPTIBLE adj. *open to, subject to, or responsive to; impressionable; liable*

I tan easily, so I didn't believe I was *susceptible* to a bad sunburn. Wrong again, Ted. That same camp-out taught me that I had an extreme *susceptibility* to poison ivy, too.

CID/CIS = to cut; to kill

concise—*short and to the point; succinct; admirably brief*
>   a *concise*, effective speech
>   with delightful *conciseness*

incisive—*decisive, direct, and forceful in approach*
>   an *incisive* analysis
>   an *incisive* decision-maker

Also: **decide, decisive, incise, incision, excise, excision, precise, precision, homicide, fratricide, matricide**

RESIGNATION n. *acceptance of the inevitable or the obvious; submissiveness, surrender; formal notice of leaving a job or a responsibility*

Mom is finally *resigned* to the idea that I'll be working out of town this summer. "Your last summer at home," she said, with a sigh of weary *resignation*. "Parents *resign* themselves to the fact that kids grow and go—but it happens so fast."

SPORADIC adj. *occurring off and on; inconstant*
Dad said, "Ted'll be home *sporadically* over the summer." "You can count on me, Ma," I assured her. "It won't be *sporadic* either. I need to do laundry and eat real food at least every other weekend."

MEMORY FIX

Need we say it? Write them, stare at them, write their meanings, say them aloud.

SUBSTITUTION Answers on page 254

> **Replace each *italicized* word or phrase with the correct word from List 25.**

1 You should consult all the club members, not just make a(n) *tyrannical* decision. _____

2 I was leafing through the anthology in a *random, unplanned* way when I found an incredible poem. _____

3 Spilling that after-shave lotion on my dresser was *extremely harmful* to the oak finish. _____

4 My mind must have wandered during the math test, because I made a *badly noticeable* error on an easy problem. _____

5 We may be *forced to face the inevitable* to our principal's leaving, but we don't have to like it. _____

6 I made some *off and on* attempts to pick up my room, but I got distracted and never finished. _____

7 The bee doesn't really flit in a(n) *unsteady, whimsical* way from flower to flower; she just looks disorganized. _____

8 Reggie's always advertising his store in such a *loud, embarrassingly pushy* way that I would never shop there. _____

9 It's tough to accept the idea of our *innately imperfect* nature until you watch toddlers push each other around. _____

10 Somebody should teach our manager how to deliver a(n) *decisively cutting to the heart of the matter* speech. _____

TRUE OR FALSE   Answers on page 254

> **Read each sentence to see how the words in List 25 are being used. Then mark T (true) or F (false) beside each.**

1 If you wore a little asafetida bag the way kids did in "the old days," you wouldn't be *susceptible* to colds. _____

2 Teachers enjoy students who *flagrantly* flout school rules. _____

3 The Pony Express would have been more efficient if it had operated in a more *desultory* or *capricious* manner. _____

4 A landscaper with an inherently *devious* mind could prove to be a natural designer of garden mazes. _____

5 My painfully shy, withdrawn Aunt Willy would have communicated better with a more *incisive* psychologist. _____

6 Snakes and mice are naturally *compatible*. _____

MATCHING Answers on page 244

> **Circle the two words or phrases that best explain the meaning of each word in bold type.**

1 **coherent** sticky logical buddy lucid inaudible

2 **concise** succinct clear cohesive brief meager

3 **devious** putrid criminal roundabout unattractive crafty

4 **compatible** agreeable comfortable positive well-suited convivial

5 **susceptible** underdone ailing confused by liable receptive to

6 **extraneous** irrelevant nonessential critical central abundant

7 **inherent** hairless hirsute inborn basic natural

8 **blatant** delayed "loud" hereditary glaring stupid

9 **sporadic** moldy druggie topmost story irregular inconstant

10 **arbitrary** despotic mediating impulsive convenient selective

189

REVIEW: LISTS 21–25

The preceding five lists featured words you'll use for the rest of your life . . . and maybe on the SAT in a few weeks. Read each of those lists again to refresh your memory before completing this oh-so-helpful review.

ANALOGIES Answers on page 244

Choose the one word pair in each list below that expresses the same relationship as the pair in capital letters.

1 TIME : ANACHRONISTIC

(A) era : mesozoic
(B) place : ubiquitous
(C) theory : hypothetical
(D) setting : incongruous
(E) country : utopian

2 PROPHET : CLAIRVOYANT

(A) tyrant : frugal
(B) paradigm : exemplary
(C) instructor : incisive
(D) architect : ethical
(E) iconoclast : vindictive

3 APPARENT : FLAGRANT

(A) brief : concise
(B) ubiquitous : omnipresent
(C) detrimental : harmful
(D) careful : assiduous
(E) sporadic : desultory

4 WATER : TURBULENT

(A) knowledge : esoteric
(B) excuse : extenuating
(C) decision : imprudent
(D) reason : unethical
(E) thought : incoherent

5 APPETITE : VORACIOUS

(A) milk : homogeneous
(B) apparel : voluminous
(C) mind : oblivious
(D) route : devious
(E) talent : minimal

6 EXTRANEOUS : DETAIL

(A) peripheral : issue
(B) animated : cartoon
(C) elusive : enigma
(D) generic : drug
(E) ingenuous : idea

FIND THE ODDBALL   Answers on page 254

> In each word group, cross out the oddball—the one unrelated word or phrase.

1 genetic   gentleman   ingenious   brilliant   congenial

2 destiny   kismet   karma   predestination   fate   prophecy

3 conjectural   theoretical   hypothetical   pragmatic

4 fleeting   elusive   evasive   running   slippery

5 intending evil   malignant   swiftly powerful   virulent   hideous

6 unscathed   not touched   fragile   uninjured   harmful

191

7 spark   ignite   energize   elucidate   kindle   excite

8 alternate   discourage   inhibit   hinder   deter

9 erroneous   rash   impetuous   precipitate
headlong

10 indigent   brazen   tasteless   loud   blatant   showy

11 crooked   cunning   twisted   indirect   devious
inspired

12 forceful   direct   decisive   incisive   reclusive

WHO SAID THAT? Answers on page 245

> **From the choices offered, select the type of
> speaker for each of the following comments.**

pragmatist   credulous one   clairvoyant   pious one
eccentric   arbitrary one   iconoclast   vindictive one
convivial soul

1 There, but for the grace of God, go I.
_____

2 Oil paints are a silly tradition; I paint with mud.
_____

3 You will go on a long journey. _____

4 How about a little dessert before dinner?
_____

5 Why? Because I said so! (All parents are eventually driven to this, you know.) _____

6 Very sensible approach. I like it. _____

7 The ad promised I'd lose 10 pounds in five days. _____

8 I'll get you for that. _____

9 Yo, Goombah, let's party! _____

FIND THE SYNONYMS

Answers on page 245

> **From the word list below, choose two more synonyms to complete each group.**

chimerical	frugal	propensity	desultory	tenuous
enigmatic	congenial	fanciful	parochial	cryptic
whimsical	thrifty	tendency	capricious	narrow
tacit	flimsy	compatible	haphazard	unspoken

1 like-minded _____ sociable _____

2 inconstant _____ fanciful _____

3 random _____ unplanned _____

4 obscure _____ mysterious _____

5 sparing _____ prudent _____

6 provincial _____ limited _____

7 insubstantial _____ slight _____

8 silent _____ understood _____

9 natural leaning _____ inclination _____

10 imaginary _____ improbable _____

THE ROOT OF IT ALL Answers on page 255

Here's the root, with a blank for every missing
letter and a definition for a clue.

1 _ _ hes _ _ _   gluey or sticky

2 gen _ _ _   brilliant person

3 _ _ gen _ _ _ _   innocent, naive, gullible

4 gen _   transmitter of hereditary factors

5 _ _ gen _ _ _   to foster, begin

6 gen _ _ _ _   of a general type or class

7 _ _ _ _ _ gen _ _ _ _   faking honesty

8 cred _ _ _ _   worthy of being believed

9 _ _ _ _ _ ced _   to mediate between disputants

10 chron _ _   habitual, long-lasting

11 anim _ _ _ _ _   bitter antagonism

12 _ _ _ anim _ _ _   of a balanced, even disposition

13 _ _ sid _ _ _ _   dangerously alluring; subtle

14 _ _ ten _ _ _ _ _ _ reducing in severity or importance

15 _ _ cis _ _ _   cutting teeth

LIST 26 BOLSTER, DON'T CARP

exhaust • enervate • carp • coerce • bolster • belittle • advocate • cajole • facilitate • denounce • deplete • alienate

EXHAUST v. *to use up entirely; deplete; to wear out physically* adj. **exhaustive,** *thorough*
Nothing is more *exhausting* than college applications. My brain *exhausted* all of its ideas for essays on the first few schools. Also, each form requires such an *exhaustive* roundup of information that it would *exhaust* anyone's patience.

ENERVATE v. *to drain of energy and mental quickness*
Totally *enervated* after spending hours on these applications, I sacked out for a little power nap. Filling in miles of forms had been *enervating* beyond belief.

CARP v. *to nag in a petty, nitpicky way; to find fault*
I woke up to hear Mom *carping* about the applications being due right now. "Hey, Ma," I said when I could get a word in, "don't *carp* at me. I'm working, I'm working!"

COERCE v. *to force or compel (someone or something)*
"We can't *coerce* you into hurrying," Mom said, "but it's so much smarter to turn the applications in early. Sorry about the nagging. *Coercion* isn't our style here, you know."

BOLSTER v. *to act as a support or prop; to reinforce*
I was feeling pretty sorry for myself, so I said, "Yeah, I need major *bolstering* right now, not criticism. Being a senior is tough; we all need to be *bolstered* now and then."

BELITTLE v. *to make fun of or reduce in importance; to disparage or decry*
"Oh, boo hoo," Mom said, grinning. "I hate to *belittle* your problems, but you could be worse off—such as

195

> **CAP/CIP/CEPT = to take, get**
>
> **incipient**—*beginning to be; commencing*
> > an *incipient* cold
> > the *incipient* signs of spring
>
> **perceptive**—*keenly observant; discerning; very understanding*
> > my most *perceptive* friend
> > a *perceptive* analysis
>
> Also: **capture, captivate, caption, anticipate, reciprocate, emancipate, intercept, receptive, susceptible**

not graduating and not going to college. Still, you'll never find me *belittling* the work those applications take."

ADVOCATE v. *to support, recommend, be in favor of* n. *a person who pleads a case; lawyer*
Coming from Mom, who's always been my staunchest *advocate*, that was okay, but not terrific. However, she *advocates* total honesty within the family, and that's what I got.

CAJOLE v. *to beg earnestly, to wheedle or coax*
Hoping to *cajole* her into helping, I said, "I could really use just a teensy bit of—" and watched her shake her head. "No amount of *cajolery* will work this time. If you can't do the applications, you aren't ready for those schools."

FACILITATE v. *to make easier or simpler, to smooth the way*
"To *facilitate* your process," Mom suggested, "try using the school memories book that we've always kept. You'll get ideas from way back in kindergarten, and I'm sure that will *facilitate* the writing of all those essays."

DENOUNCE v. *to criticize, especially publicly; to accuse* n. **denunciation,** *negative criticism*
The record book was a great help, but inwardly I found myself *denouncing* college applications on all counts. It was a truly exhaustive *denunciation*; I didn't leave out any of the parts that I thought were most annoying.

DEPLETE v. *to greatly reduce any supply; to drain, bankrupt, or impoverish* n. **depletion**
By the time I finished all seven sets of forms, I had *depleted* my store of memories, my list of accomplishments, and my supply of good humor. My enthusiasm for going away to college had suffered some *depletion*, too, but it soon returned to bolster my spirits.

FER = to carry, bear, bring

infer—*to conclude from available evidence; to deduce, guess*
> *infer* his meaning from his tone
> can *infer* when he's tired

proliferate—*to multiply, increase rapidly in number*
> cancerous cells that *proliferate*
> a *proliferation* of schools

Also: **confer, conference, vociferous, transfer, coniferous** *(cone-bearing),* **proffer, offer, defer, deference**

ALIENATE v. *to estrange, set apart by ill will (affections or people who had once been close)*
On discovering that I was one of the few who had finished all of his college applications, I kept quiet for fear of *alienating* my friends. Usually, I'd rather not mention something than *alienate* people.

MEMORY FIX
Once again, write each word you don't know, with a definition for each, then say the words aloud.

197

FILL IN THE BLANKS Answers on page 255

> From the new words in List 26, select the one that best completes the meaning and logic of each sentence. Change the form of the word as required for correctness.

1 A long hike is _____ for the trained hiker only if some emergency forces him to _____ his energy early in the hike.

2 I don't mean to _____ your work, but picking up your room will probably not make the *Guinness Book of Records.*

3 Our family's tired of the constantly _____ critics on TV and in newspapers, who apparently never approve of anyone or anything.

4 We stayed with Amy until she went into surgery, hoping to _____ her spirits about losing her wisdom teeth.

5 "I can _____ from the look of your faces," she said, "that I'm not going to feel so hot when the anesthetic wears off."

6 Ever since she was little, Amy's been unusually _____ when it comes to reading faces.

7 General anesthesia drains me of energy for days afterward, so for me it has a seriously _____ effect.

8 In the dental recovery room, I could detect small bulges in Amy's cheeks, _____ signs of the swelling to come.

9 Hoping to _____ recovery by reducing swelling and pain, we held ice packs to Amy's cheeks.

10 No amount of _____ would have made Amy eat those first hours after surgery, but eventually we _____ her into drinking a milkshake.

ANTONYMS Answers on page 255

> You'll recognize some of these antonyms from past lists as you make the match of opposites.

_____	**1.** bolster	acclaim
_____	**2.** deplete	energize
_____	**3.** denounce	dull, obtuse
_____	**4.** incipient	contain
_____	**5.** facilitate	undermine
_____	**6.** perceptive	extol
_____	**7.** enervate	terminal, final
_____	**8.** proliferate	hamper, hinder
_____	**9.** carp	replenish

199

SWITCHEROO

Answers on page 255

Many words in this lesson, in addition to being verbs, are also nouns and adjectives. Match these equally important words with their meanings.

_____ **1.** alienation   supporter

_____ **2.** advocacy   keenness

_____ **3.** depletion   conclusion, deduction

_____ **4.** perceptiveness   estrangement

_____ **5.** advocate   wheedling, begging

_____ **6.** proliferation   force

_____ **7.** inference   sponsorship, support

_____ **8.** denunciation   exhaustion

_____ **9.** cajolery   (rapid) multiplication

_____ **10.** coercion   negative criticism

HOW BIZARRE!

bizarre • prosaic • zany • static • urbane •
opaque • stoic • subtle • latent • innate •
futile • candid

BIZARRE adj. *strikingly unusual or incongruous; fantastic or jolting in impact*
Our word *bizarre* was once *bizarro*, Spanish for "brave" or "handsome," and also *bizar* for the Basques, who greatly admired beards. Not the French; they loathed beards and termed the Basques *bizarre*, meaning "strange."

PROSAIC adj. *ordinary, unexciting, dull, unimaginative*
I've led an awfully predictable, *prosaic* life so far. I'd like to do a year of college studies abroad, which would be foreign and exciting, not at all *prosaic*.

ZANY adj. *wacky, absurd, ludicrous, "crazy"*
Zany, a nickname for Giovanni (John), was a common way to address servants in sixteenth-century Italy. In their local plays, a clowning servant was a *Zani*, who always made a fool of his master. What a *zany* history for a word!

STATIC adj. *unchanging; quiet, at rest; stationary, fixed;* n. *electronic noise; back talk (slang)*
The last chem experiment concerned solutions that remained *static* in spite of various attempts to destabilize them. When you think about it, not much in life remains *static*.

URBANE adj. *smooth and sophisticated (said of men); suave*
From the Latin *urbs* (city) comes *urbane* to describe a polished city fellow, the opposite of a country hick. Once, actor David Niven was considered the epitome of the *urbane* male. (Watch the video of *Around the World in 80 Days*.)

ANTHROP = man, human being

misanthrope—*one who hates people or distrusts them*
>   the attitudes of a confirmed *misanthrope*

philanthropy—*generous donation of time or money to benefit others (lit. love for human beings)*
>   the famous *philanthropist* Andrew Carnegie

Also: **anthropoid, anthropology, anthropomorphism**

OPAQUE adj. *difficult to explain or to understand; mentally slow, obtuse, thick-skulled; also, not allowing light to pass through* n. **opacity**
The beautiful characters that make up the Chinese and the Japanese languages often appear daunting, even *opaque* to Westerners like me. I hate to think that I'm the one who's *opaque*, so I'll probably try to learn Japanese in college.

STOIC adj. *showing no feeling or pain; impassive*
Taking their name from the porch (*stoa*) where they met, the old Greek *Stoics* were taught by Zeno to be indifferent to passion or pain and to accept calmly whatever happened in life. People who could *stoically* ignore pain probably fared much better in ancient times.

SUBTLE adj. *not obvious in any way; elusive; hard to understand (as "a subtle language"); keenly discerning (as "subtle interpretation"); extremely clever; behaving in an insidious way (as "a subtle disease")*
Both cancer and AIDS are diseases feared for their *subtlety*. Scores of the country's *subtlest* medical minds are concentrated on these dreaded ailments.

LATENT adj. *hidden, submerged, waiting to be aroused or discovered; inactive, dormant, potential*
Throughout school, I kept hoping that good coaching would uncover a *latent* talent for some sport, preferably wrestling. But whatever I've got in the way of *latent* ability is still dormant, so now I'm looking for a sport that's just fun.

INNATE adj. *inborn, inherent, natural*
An *innately* talented composer, Mozart wrote music with skill and confidence before age 5. In the

remaining thirty years of his life, he created over 600 compositions, many of which have an *innate* perfection of form that remains unmatched.

AC/ACR = sharp

acute—*sharp or pointed; keenly perceptive (as "an acute eye")*
> an *acute* commentary
> family known for their *acute* minds

acrimonious—*bitterly sharp, rancorous, biting*
> an unusually *acrimonious* remark
> based on *acrimony*

exacerbate—*to make (a condition) worse; to aggravate*
> don't *exacerbate* that sprain
> illness *exacerbated* by worry

Also: **acrid, acrimony, acerbic, acumen** (All SAT favorites!)

FUTILE adj. *ineffective, useless; vain (as "a futile hope")* n. **futility** (*Note:* utile = useful)
I've wasted a lot of time in *futile* tasks, such as trying to keep my room neat. I'm going to abandon this exercise in *futility*, because the room feels weird when it's too tidy.

CANDID adj. *honest, open, without guile or deceit; frank, even blunt* n. **candor**
Poet George Canning wrote, "Save, save, oh save me from the *candid* friend!" as a reminder that it's possible to be too frank with someone close to you. Sometimes a friend needs more thoughtfulness and a lot less *candor*.

MEMORY FIX
Here we go again. Write down each word you don't know; write its meaning, and say each one aloud.

203

TRUE OR FALSE
Answers on page 255

Read each sentence below to see how the new words in List 26 are being used. Then mark T (true) or F (false) beside each one.

1 The best tone for a thank-you note is one of *acrimony*. _____

2 More rain will only *exacerbate* our current drought. _____

3 You'd better hope your dentist is not a *misanthrope*. _____

4 No one ever exhibits a trained rabbit, leading us to infer that bunnies are not overly *acute*. _____

5 "Mind over matter" is an apt motto for the *stoic*. _____

6 Many allegedly *futile* projects, such as going to the moon, have been accomplished; more will probably follow. _____

7 The opposite of misanthropy is *philanthropy*. _____

8 The caveman's stout club was proof of his innate *subtlety*. _____

9 Prepare to put on a *stoic* face if someone begins a conversation like this: "In all *candor* I feel I must tell you that. . . ." _____ _____

204

10 Chances are, everyone has *latent* abilities.

_____

FIND THE SYNONYMS Answers on page 255

> **From the word list below, add the correct synonyms to each numbered group by writing them on the appropriate lines.**

dull-witted	inborn	guileless	suave	ordinary
unimaginative	insidious	shocking	potential	ludicrous
very clever	dormant	absurd	inherent	fantastic
sophisticated	obtuse	unchanging	frank	stationary

1 bizarre   incongruous   odd

_____   _____

2 prosaic   dull   humdrum

_____   _____

3 zany   wacko   crazy

_____   _____

4 static   fixed   quiet

_____   _____

5 urbane   polished   smooth

_____   _____

6 opaque   hard to penetrate or understand

_____   _____

7 subtle   elusive   very discerning

_____   _____

8 latent   hidden   inactive

_____   _____

9 innate natural

_____ _____

10 candid open honest

_____ _____

SUBSTITUTION Answers on page 255

> **For the words or phrases in *italics*, substitute the correct words from List 27.**

1 There's nothing *dull or commonplace* about that checkout girl; it's an orangutan in a(n) *outlandish* costume. _____ _____

2 He may be a(n) *polished*, well-dressed fellow, but under that designer haircut is an exceedingly *dim-witted* brain. _____ _____

3 The *frank, open* comments of that hockey player with the *impervious to pain* look on his face led to a(n) *bitterly cutting* exchange. _____ _____

4 Don't give me any *negative noise* on that decision. _____

5 We've suggested that our *wacko* Aunt Jolly change her ways, but it's *useless* to even talk to her. _____ _____

quizzical • rigorous • reprehensible • salutary • prolific • recalcitrant • pedestrian • unassailable • volatile • superfluous • obsolete • diffident

QUIZZICAL adj. *teasing, but questioning too; puzzled*
"You're in charge of Senior Weekend?" Mom said with a *quizzical* look. "Tell me you're kidding!" Of course, I wasn't teasing, and her look went from *quizzical* to concerned.

RIGOROUS adj. *demanding or strict in requirements; absolutely accurate and precise; harsh (climate)*

"We'll expect you to keep *rigorous* accounts of all your expenses," the senior adviser told me. Any way I looked at it, I had taken on an extremely *rigorous* task.

REPREHENSIBLE adj. *deserving blame or criticism*
Then I had a *reprehensible* thought: What if I said I couldn't plan Senior Weekend after all? What was really *reprehensible* of me—and just plain dumb—was thinking that I could do this job without a committee of helpers.

SALUTARY adj. *promoting good health (mental or physical)*
The idea of helpers was so *salutary* that I cheered up and went in search of a committee. The five of us met over burgers and fries—tasty, though not very *salutary*—to discuss ideas for the weekend after graduation.

PROLIFIC adj. *very productive or fruitful; fertile, fecund*
Prolific critters such as mice and rabbits produce an impressive number of progeny. So do *prolific* minds

FLU/FLUX/FLUCT = to flow

mellifluous—*sweetly or smoothly flowing (of sounds or voices)*

> a *mellifluous* vocalist
> instrument with *mellifluous* tones

fluent—*gifted in speaking; graceful in movement; polished*

> a *fluent* speaker of French
> the *fluent* body of a gymnast

Also: **affluent, fluid, fluctuate, influence, confluence, effluent, effluvium, influx, flux, fluxion**

create ideas; my committee suggested so many that we had trouble deciding what to do.

RECALCITRANT adj. *very tough to control; defiant of authority; unruly, refractory*
Four of us agreed on a great idea, but one *recalcitrant* kid said no. As I wondered how to win him over, I remembered that he'd been pretty stubborn and *recalcitrant* ever since kindergarten.

PEDESTRIAN adj. *commonplace, ordinary, unimaginative; referring to going by foot (as "a pedestrian walk")*
"Renting an old, broken-down camp for the weekend," Harold grumbled. "That's so ho-hum . . . so *pedestrian*! For once, can't we do something that isn't so boringly *pedestrian*?"

UNASSAILABLE adj. *not assailable; not open to attack, to question, or to doubt*
Jodie grinned. "Pedestrian, huh? Well, troops, we now have *unassailable* proof that Harold prepped for SATs." "Very funny," he retorted. "Also *unassailable* is the fact that we still haven't got a good idea!"

VOLATILE adj. *quick to express emotion; explosive, easily triggered (a chemical or a person's temper); changeable, unstable*
Now here's a *volatile* guy for you, I thought, wondering why I hadn't remembered Harold's quick temper. The other aspect of his *volatility*, however, was changeability, and as Jodie kept talking, Harold came around.

SUPERFLUOUS adj. *extra, unnecessary; or, wasteful*

Harold said, "Okay, just a few questions. First, and this is major, not *superfluous*, what are we going to do for two days? That camp barely has electricity, you know!" True, and electricity isn't exactly a *superfluous* item.

SPIC/SPEC/SPECT = to look, see

conspicuous—*very noticeable; commanding attention, striking*

> *conspicuous* by his absence
> a *conspicuous* display of talent

circumspect—*cautious, watchful, careful, and prudent*

> take the time needed for a *circumspect* decision

Also: **auspicious, suspicion, perspicacity, perspicuous, spectator, inspection, speculation, specious**

OBSOLETE adj. *out of date, not in use; outmoded, passé*

I'd forgotten that the camp's equipment was *obsolete*. Of course, I'd been thinking about the lake and the dock and the canoes, things that would never be *obsolete* for me.

DIFFIDENT adj. *hesitant, lacking confidence; unassertive*

"Well," I began *diffidently*, a new idea taking hold, "let's rough it, then. No electricity, no boom boxes—not one modern thing. Total nostalgia," I continued happily, my *diffident* attitude vanishing. "That wouldn't be pedestrian!"

MEMORY FIX

Of course you remember. Write the words you don't know with their definitions. Say them aloud and THINK.

FIND THE ODDBALL Answers on page 255

In each word group, cross out the oddball—the one unrelated word or phrase.

1 proficient with language   fluent   skillful   articulate

2 dangerous   explosive   changeable   volatile   unstable

3 charming   smooth   richly flowing   mellifluous

4 unconfident   diffident   unsure   wary   unaggressive

5 hard to manage   pedestrian   naughty   defiant   unruly

MATCHING Answers on page 256

In column B, find two synonyms or phrases that explain each word in column A. Write them on the lines provided.

	A	B
_____	**1.** recalcitrant	prudent
_____		unnecessary
_____	**2.** circumspect	outmoded
_____		unimaginative
_____	**3.** diffident	refractory
_____		striking
_____	**4.** obsolete	totally accurate
_____		hesitant

_____ **5.** rigorous   productive

_____   fertile

_____ **6.** prolific   wasteful

_____   passé

_____ **7.** pedestrian   watchful

_____   demanding

_____ **8.** conspicuous   unassertive

_____   unruly

_____ **9.** superfluous   very noticeable

_____   ordinary

FILL IN THE BLANKS Answers on page 256

Select the best word from List 28 to complete the meaning and logic of each sentence. Change any word as needed for grammatical correctness.

1 Obviously puzzled as to my meaning, yet trying not to laugh, Jeff gave me a _____ glance and waited for my reply.

2 The pilot maintained he could fly anything, even the most _____ propeller plane in the hangar.

3 As a result of the massive data compiled during that study, their conclusions are virtually _____ .

211

4 A brisk walk is one traditional way of starting the day in a _____ way.

5 For the person who's done something _____ , there's an old saying: "Confession is good for the soul."

6 Valiant soldiers are decorated for _____ bravery.

7 A typical European, _____ in at least two or three languages, puts most Americans to shame.

8 _____ outdoor programs like Outward Bound have proved to be effective at building self-esteem.

9 Janie's is the sweetest voice in the world, the only _____ one in the midst of that cacophony of noise.

10 A moody, _____ person is apt to erupt like Pinatubo.

LIST 29 ATTITUDES

aloof • partisan • demeanor • altruism •
austere • provincial • authoritarian •
nonchalant • brusque • contrite •
conciliatory • spurious

ALOOF adj. *reserved or cool in manner; uninvolved, remote*
Nearly 200 years ago, Coleridge wrote: "*Aloof* with hermit-eye I scan / The present works of present man— / A wild and dreamlike trade of blood and guile, / Too foolish for a tear, too wicked for a smile." Looks as if it's always been tough to remain *aloof* from the evil that people keep creating.

PARTISAN adj. *strongly in favor, biased, prejudiced* n. *follower or member*

In a country tired of *partisan* politics, the American electorate hungers for representatives who will put the good of the country, not their political party, first. Many voters feel that pure *partisan* voting is blind voting.

DEMEANOR n. *manner of handling yourself; mien, comportment, bearing*
Queens are often described as having a stately *demeanor*, and busy officials have a bustling *demeanor*. Our *demeanor* is our body language and a major clue to character.

ALTRUISM n. *unselfish giving for the benefit of others*
Society has some full-time *altruists*, like teaching nuns and priests or Peace Corps volunteers, and now and then the rest of us are motivated by *altruism*. Major religions are based on the *altruistic* concept that those who give will receive.

AUSTERE adj. *reserved, grave, somber in manner; self-denying, abstemious; restrained* n. **austerity**

FID = faith

infidel—*a disbeliever in some specific sense*
> declared him an *infidel* and banned him
> from the church

perfidy—*faithlessness, disloyalty; betrayal, treachery*
> hated for his *perfidy*
> what *perfidious* behavior

Also: **confide, confidence, fidelity, diffident, diffidence, affidavit, confidant** *(intimate, trusted friend)*

People who devote their lives to others aren't self-indulgent, so the altruistic life is often quite *austere*. One example of holy *austerity* is that of the contemplative monks who work and meditate in silence, talking only rarely.

PROVINCIAL adj. *referring to the provinces, or country; unsophisticated; or, parochial, narrow* n. provincial

Abraham Lincoln was once scorned as a *provincial* fellow by those who equated sophistication with intelligence. That same error was made in the fable of the city mouse who thought his country cousin was a *provincial*.

AUTHORITARIAN adj. *favoring subservience or allegiance to an authority rather than personal independence or freedom*

Author Edmund Wilson said, "Marx and Engels, coming out of *authoritarian* Germany, tended to imagine socialism in *authoritarian* terms." Independent Americans, of course, are never very comfortable with *authoritarian* governments.

NONCHALANT adj. *casual, carefree, cool, unconcerned*

Nonchalant at first, our family shrugged and said, "Oh, well, we can probably live with a few bats in the attic." But that *nonchalance* vanished when we began to smell something.

BRUSQUE adj. *curt, abrupt, blunt (unpleasant in effect)*

When I said I needed to get rid of some bats in our attic, the clerk at the bat and bird shop snapped *brusquely,* "You should appreciate bats." Put off by her *brusque* manner, I said I was crazy about them, but not in my house.

ERR = to wander

erratic—*on no set course, wandering, nomadic; devious*
> the *erratic* path of the butterfly
> at *erratic* intervals

aberration—*eccentricity; an oddity, not the norm*
> signs of an *aberrant* mind
> the *aberrations* of a recluse

Also: **error, erroneous, errant, arrant** *(extreme)*

CONTRITE adj. *sorrowful or repentant for some wrong* n. **contrition**
We're going to evict the bats from our house if we can, and we will not feel *contrite*. Well, maybe we'll suffer a few momentary pangs of *contrition*, but the bats can move to a nearby belfry.

CONCILIATORY adj. *reconciling, appeasing, pacifying (to improve relations)* v. **conciliate**
As a *conciliatory* gesture to the bats, I opened the louvers on the belfry of our church, advertising its desirability as a bat residence. I don't mind *conciliating* bats, who consume zillions of annoying bugs and mosquitoes.

SPURIOUS adj. *false, fake, though appearing legitimate; forged (as "a spurious passport")*
Opening the louvers to promote our church belfry as a home for the bats was not *spurious* advertising, because bats have always liked belfries. Generally speaking, though, the world of advertising generates a fair number of *spurious* claims.

MEMORY FIX
Very near the end now. . . . Write down each word you don't know well; write definitions for each. Say them aloud.

215

FILL IN THE BLANKS Answers on page 256

> **From the new words in List 29 select the one that best completes the meaning and logic of each phrase. Use the correct form of each word.**

1 moved with the regal _____ of a Paris model

2 tossed his head _____ as if it didn't matter to him

3 ordered us to leave in a most _____ manner

4 Vidkun Quisling, a traitor whose _____ resulted in his surname becoming a word

5 following the wild, _____ path of the fleeing rabbit

6 apologizing for the omission with a sincere, _____ smile

7 illegal immigrants entering the United States with _____ documents

8 made timid by her _____, forbidding countenance

9 a generous person, known for a life of _____

10 eager to make up, extending his hand in a _____ gesture

216

WHO SAID THAT?

Answers on page 256

From the list below, choose the most likely speaker to go with each remark.

an infidel	a partisan	the brusque type
the provincial	the authoritarian	an austere person
an altruist	a perfidious one	a nonchalant one

1 I have no need of jewelry or stylish clothes or elegantly prepared foods. The simple life suits me. _____

2 We don't have to deal with that out here where there's a mile between neighbors, you see? _____

3 Briefly, that's it. Don't get it? Tough. _____

4 I am my brother's keeper. _____

5 They aren't like us—not at all, no sir. Why they should be so different from us is beyond me. _____

6 I'm not wearing that thing over my face and walking meekly behind him; you can just forget it! _____

7 Just do what I said and don't ask questions. _____

8 I leaked that information, and I'd do it again. _____

9 No sweat. Don't let it bother you. _____

TRUE OR FALSE   Answers on page 256

> **Read each sentence to see how the new words in List 29 are being used. Then mark T (true) or F (false) beside each one.**

1 To Americans, cannibalism is more than a mere *aberration*. _____

2 For the sake of our teachers, we should turn in assignments on an *erratic* basis. _____

3 Neutral nations avoid entanglements, remaining *aloof*. _____

4 After bopping your brother on the head, you should assume a *contrite demeanor* and apologize. _____

5 The psychologist who masters a *brusque* approach will be the most successful. _____

6 One of the better *conciliatory* lines is, "We'll make sure that doesn't happen again." _____

7 To think that only private schools can offer a good education is a *provincial* outlook. _____

8 A *bipartisan* committee will probably write the Republican platform for the next election. _____

218

negligence • deleterious • depravity • crass • morose • caustic • guile • clandestine • cynical • furtive • apprehension • decadence

NEGLIGENCE n. *lack of a sensible amount of care; neglect, carelessness* adj. **negligent**
Having bats in your house is not a sign of *negligence*, as bats can enter through the tiniest of openings. Learning that we hadn't been *negligent* homeowners helped us to feel somewhat better about the bats in our attic.

DELETERIOUS adj. *causing harm or injury, maybe in a very subtle way; maybe pernicious (deadly)*
We began to fret about the *deleterious* effects the bats might have on our house. One especially *deleterious* result of their invasion was the steady accumulation of bat guano.

DEPRAVITY n. *a state of corruption, perversion, or evil* adj. **depraved**
Grinning, Dad said, "I suggest we bag that stuff and sell it for fertilizer . . . if you don't think that's too *depraved*." Hearing our quite well-mannered father link himself to *depravity* made us hoot with laughter.

CRASS adj. *utterly lacking in taste or discrimination*
"I hate to sound *crass*," Mom interrupted, "but what do you think we could get for a bag of bat poo?" Coming from her, that was a *crass* remark, all right, but awfully funny.

MOROSE adj. *very gloomy or sullen in manner*
Amy stared *morosely* at the floor. Finally she said, "Look at me, troops. This is a depressed person wearing a *morose* face because we've got a real problem and you're all acting wacko!"

CAUSTIC adj. *biting, incisive, cutting, corrosive*

BEL/BELL = war

belligerent—*combative, liking to start fights, bellicose*

> a *belligerent* attitude
> historically *belligerent* nations

rebellious—*resisting or opposing authority, refractory, recalcitrant*

> a *rebellious* attitude that always led to trouble

Also: **rebel, rebellion, antebellum** *(before the Civil War)* [And also **bell = beauty**—*belle, embellish*]

That was a pretty *caustic* approach for Amy, but her bedroom is right under the bats' roosting area. I guess I'd have a few *caustic* comments myself if my room were that close to the bat colony.

GUILE n. *trickery or deceit; deceptive cunning; duplicity*

Eventually, our family agreed that, although we liked bats and benefited from their insect-eating prowess, we would use every bit of *guile* we had to evict them. No strangers to cunning, bats are *guileful* creatures themselves at times.

CLANDESTINE adj. *secret, surreptitious*

Of course, I had already made a *clandestine* trip to our church belfry to open the louvres wider, hoping to lure the bats into the belfry. I'd been deliberately *clandestine* about my mission at church, because it sounded weird.

CYNICAL adj. *distrustful of human nature; pessimistic, even misanthropic*

"I hate to be *cynical*," Dad said, "but how do you know that our bats will want to move to a belfry?" Of course I didn't know, and I was having deeply *cynical* thoughts myself about our ability to convince the bats to move out.

FURTIVE adj. *on the sly, in secret; surreptitious; stolen*

I zipped upstairs for a *furtive* peek at my old encyclopedia. Reading those basic bat facts again gave me an idea. There would be another *furtive* trip, I decided, this time to the bats' attic home, with an ultrasound device in hand.

VERS/VERT = to turn

diverge—*to alter a course; to go apart from one point; to differ in opinion; to deviate; to swerve*

    diverging rays of sunlight

    attitude *diverged* from the norm

diverse—*unlike, different*

    went their *diverse* ways

    several *diverse* opinions on that

Also: **revert, overt, covert, versatile, inadvertant, divert, diversion, perverse, controversy, extrovert, introvert**

APPREHENSION n. *a foreboding of something bad; or, legal arrest*

Wishing I felt less *apprehension*, I prayed that the bats would move away from the electronic jamming of their radar. And what if they didn't? I waited *apprehensively* for the worst—Dad's call to an exterminator—but bats are smart, and ours soon moved next door to the belfry.

DECADENCE n. *decline and decay; deterioration*

We didn't have a totally *decadent* party after the bats left; I mean, we didn't really fall apart, but it was a loud, late party. Our neighbors made some not-too-subtle comments about how noisy it must have been in old, *decadent* Rome.

MEMORY FIX

For the last time! Write down each word you don't know well along with a definition for each. Say them aloud.

WORDS IN CONTEXT

Answers on page 256

> **Write the meanings of the words in *italics* on the lines provided.**

1 Arranging a *clandestine* meeting with the current love of your life is okay, but if you plan a *furtive* meeting, I'll be *apprehensive*, because *furtive* has more negative connotations.

_____ _____ _____

2 It's no surprise to learn that a *depraved* lifestyle has *deleterious* effects on health. _____

_____

3 History tells us that the *decadence* of Rome led to its decline. _____

4 Stung by several of his *caustic* remarks, I belatedly reminded myself that the fellow was a well-known *cynic*. _____ _____

5 Although Americans are obviously obsessed with money, it is considered by some to be a *crass* topic. _____

6 Is there such a thing as a purely *guileless* soul? _____

7 Mouth set in a *rebellious* pout, he remained silent. _____

8 After I accused him of gross *negligence*, he turned to me and sneered *morosely*, "So what?"

_____ _____

222

MATCHING SYNONYMS Answers on page 256

Match the words in column A with their synonyms or definitions in column B.

	A	B
_____	1. clandestine	in poor taste
_____	2. diverge	foreboding
_____	3. caustic	deterioration
_____	4. diverse	pessimistic
_____	5. apprehension	deceit
_____	6. decadence	secret
_____	7. crass	biting, corrosive
_____	8. belligerent/bellicose	to go apart
_____	9. guile	different
_____	10. cynical	spoiling for a fight

RHYME TIME Answers on page 256

Add what is needed from List 30 to these varied bits of poetry, some wonderful, some corny.

1 The English teacher's face was long and _____ .

"Oh why," she cried, "are my writers verbose?"

2 "Macavity, Macavity, there's no one like Macavity,
For he's a fiend in feline shape, a monster of _____ ."

From *Old Possum's Book of Practical Cats*, T. S. Eliot

3 Cartoon cat Tom assumes a(n) _____ air,
And we know he's tiptoeing toward Jerry's lair.

4 He said, "Let me at him," with a(n) _____ grin,

Laced up his boxing gloves and waded in.

5 "Two roads _____ in a yellow wood," begins one of the most famous pieces of poetry ever written, by Robert Frost. Beginning at one place, the two roads followed a different path, and Frost "took the one less traveled by." Remember?

224

REVIEW: LISTS 26–30

Yahoo, the last review! Read each group of words in lists 26–30 aloud and think of what each word means. Now you're ready for this final review.

ANALOGIES Answers on page 246

> Choose the one word pair in each list below that expresses the same relationship as the pair in capital letters.

1 DOCUMENT : SPURIOUS
- (A) flight : erratic
- (B) nation : decadent
- (C) outline : diverse
- (D) passport : false
- (E) effort : futile

2 RESOURCES : DEPLETE
- (A) supplies : facilitate
- (B) health : enervate
- (C) strength : exhaust
- (D) force : coerce
- (E) energy : assail

3 CARPING : ALIENATION
- (A) apprehension : foreboding
- (B) perfidy : aberration
- (C) acrimony : conciliation
- (D) partisanship : rebellion
- (E) negligence : decadence

4 MISANTHROPE : CYNICAL
- (A) pedestrian : obsolete
- (B) stoic : impassive
- (C) altruist : unassailable
- (D) philanthropist : nonchalant
- (E) zany : depraved

5 SUBTLE : COVERT

- (A) flagrant : conspicuous
- (B) latent : innate
- (C) furtive : crass
- (D) reprehensible : bizarre
- (E) austere : provincial

6 PARTISAN : ALOOF

- (A) judge : perceptive
- (B) infidel : loyal
- (C) rebel : affluent
- (D) colonel : rigorous
- (E) buyer : urbane

MATCHING ANTONYMS

Answers on page 257

> **Match the words in column A with their opposites in column B.**

	A	B
_____	1. reprehensible	deleterious
_____	2. urbane	belittle
_____	3. candid	learned, acquired
_____	4. bolster	docile
_____	5. salutary	vital
_____	6. recalcitrant	laudable
_____	7. innate	conciliatory
_____	8. austerity	self-absorption
_____	9. superfluous	coerce

_____ **10.** acrimonious   provincial

_____ **11.** cajole   guileful

_____ **12.** altruism   self-indulgence

MATCHING   Answers on page 257

Circle the two words or phrases that best explain the meaning of each numbered word in bold type.

1 fluent

orally skilled   verbose   swiftly flowing
graceful   polite

2 latent

delayed   recent   potential   dormant   lost

3 diffident

unassertive   strange   unusual   hesitant
argumentative

4 contrite

boring   banal   remorseful   repentant   angry

5 crass

gross   mean-spirited   tasteless   thoughtless
grasping

6 furtive

surreptitious   illegal   superstitious   clandestine
forbidden

7 acute

perceptive   charming   geometric   pointed   painful

8 infer

popular pine tree   conclude   resume

deduce   suppose

9 prosaic

pedestrian   enervating   tiring   everyday

unpoetic

10 authoritarian

democratic   autocratic   despotic   rigorous

demonic

> **From the list below, select the best word to
> complete each sentence. Alter the words as
> required for grammatical correctness.**

erratic   static   facilitate   aberration   caustic

advocate   diverse   rigorous   circumspect   prolific

morose   denounce   futile   bellicose

1 Trained as a biochemist, Isaac Asimov was one
of our century's most versatile, _____
authors, publishing over 300 books on
_____ topics.

2 The dynamics of a changing community assure
that almost nothing within it will remain
_____ for long.

228

3 Can anything be done to _____ the use of high-speed rail in this country, or is that a _____ cause, doomed to fail?

4 "I'm afraid the old dog's _____ heartbeat is the norm for him now, not just a temporary _____ ," said the vet.

5 It's one thing to be _____ , but Mother's Aunt Aggie is so unswervingly prudent that she never has any fun.

6 You can wipe that _____ , down-in-the-mouth look off your face with some _____ exercise that enlivens mind and body.

7 Always quick to criticize, the media have enjoyed _____ the new administration with one comment after another.

8 Some boys have such a _____ nature that counselors _____ sports like boxing to help them vent their aggression.

TRUE OR FALSE Answers on page 257

> Read the sentences below to see if the words in the past five lists are being used correctly. Then mark T (true) or F (false) beside each one.

1 Someone exhibiting a *nonchalant demeanor* in the presence of highly *volatile* substances manipulated by a *zany* fanatic can indeed be characterized as cool. _____

2 It helps if the instructions to your VCR are somewhat *opaque*. _____

229

3 *Proliferation* of nuclear weapons *exacerbates* an already *apprehensive* attitude on the part of many. _____

4 You can be *enervated* even by an *incipient* illness. _____

5 You're apt to give a *bizarre* outfit a *quizzical* look. _____

6 *Brusque* funeral home directors do a thriving business. _____

THE ANSWERS

WHAT YOU ALREADY KNOW—A QUICK REVIEW

Lesson A, Memory Check (page 11)

Prefix A/AN; Meaning: *not, without*; Examples: atheist, anomaly, atypical

Prefix AB/ABS; Meaning: *from, away*; Examples: absent, abdicate, abstain

Prefix DIS/DI/DIFF; Meaning: *away, apart, negative*; Examples: disparate, dissuade, difference

Prefix ANTE/ANTI; Meaning: *before, previous*; Examples: anteroom, anticipate

Prefix BENE; Meaning: *good, well*; Examples: benefit, benevolent, beneficial

Prefix CIRCU; Meaning: *around*; Examples: circumference, circumvent, circuit

Prefix DI/DIA; Meaning: *across, apart, through*; Examples: diameter, dialogue, dilate

Prefix ANTI; Meaning: *against, opposing*; Examples: antisocial, antidote, antipathy

Prefix CO/COL/COM; Meaning: *with, together*; Examples: cooperate, concede, concur

Lesson B, Memory Check 1 (page 12)

1. outside **2.** mixed, not all the same **3.** *in*decent and *in*substantial **4.** playing it for all you're worth, to the *maximum* **5.** bad; *maleficent* literally means *make bad* **6.** changes or alters

Lesson B, Memory Check 2 (page 14)

Prefix MICRO; Meaning: *small*; Examples: microbe, microphone, microcosm

Prefix PRE; Meaning: *before*; Examples: predict, prefix, preliminary

Prefix ORTH; Meaning: *straight, right*; Examples: orthopedic, orthodox

Prefix PER; Meaning: *through, throughout*, or *completely, wrongly*; Examples: permeate, permit

Prefix PERI; Meaning: *around, near*; Examples: periscope, perimeter, periphery

Prefix PRO; Meaning: *for, forward, before, forth, favoring*; Examples: promote, provision

Prefix POST; Meaning: *after, following*; Examples: postpone, postmortem, posterior

Prefix RE/RETRO; Meaning: *back, again*; Examples: recoil, retreat, retroactive

Prefix OMNI/PAN; Meaning: *all, entire*; Examples: omnipresent, pantheon, pandemic

Lesson B, Memory Check 3 (page 16)

1. *se*parated **2.** afar **3.** *sub*marine **4.** Super, super, *sur*pass **5.** *syn*chronizing, *together*

LIST 1
Fill in the Blanks *(page 19)*
1. acquiese   **2.** condone   **3.** effaced   **4.** chastise   **5.** concurred
6. laud   **7.** amass   **8.** augment   **9.** digress   **10.** cursory
11. digressive   **12.** coalesced   **13.** disperse   **14.** disperse
15. emitted

Analogies *(page 21)*
1. The correct answer is (C). chastise : misbehavior :: laud :
success
Implied comparison. Behaviors linked to the verbs most commonly
associated with them.
2. The correct answer is (E). footprints : efface :: record : obliterate
Implied comparison. Two human traces and ways in which they
are commonly "wiped out," completely eradicated.
3. The correct answer is (B). acquiese : yielding :: disperse :
scattering
Inherent linkage. *Acquiesce* always implies giving way or yielding,
just as *disperse* always refers to scattering in some sense.
4. The correct answer is (A). path : stray :: lecture : digress
Implied comparison. To leave a path is to *stray* off it, just as
leaving the main point of a lecture is to *digress*. These words are
linked by usage as well as by meaning.
5. The correct answer is (C). pardon : offense :: condone : error
Implied comparison. An *offense*, if excused, is said to be *pardoned*,
whereas an *error*—less serious in nature—is said to be *condoned* if
someone overlooks it or makes excuses.

Matching *(page 22)*
1. (B) assent, (D) yield
2. (A) utter, (B) voice
3. (B) chastise, (C) scold
4. (A) forerunner, (D) harbinger
5. (B) accumulate, (C) gather
6. (A) enlarge, (B) add to
7. (B) strew around, (D) disseminate
8. (A) join, (C) come together
9. (B) wear away, (C) erase
10. (A) sketchy, (D) hasty

LIST 2
True or False *(page 26)*
1. F   **2.** T   **3.** F   **4.** F   **5.** T   **6.** F   **7.** T   **8.** F   **9.** T
10. T

Matching *(page 27)*
1. d   **2.** g   **3.** l   **4.** h   **5.** i   **6.** c   **7.** e   **8.** k   **9.** a   **10.** j
11. b   **12.** f

Fill in the Blanks *(page 28)*
1. banal and hackneyed (and maybe also *trite* and full of *platitudes!*)   **2.** concise, succinct, laconic, terse, and pithy
3. hyperbole   **4.** platitude, banality   **5.** equivocal

LIST 3
Fill in the Blanks (page 32)
1. insurgents   2. hypocritical   3. hedonistic   4. glutton
5. inexorable   6. charlatans (possibly *hypocrites* or *sycophants*)
7. skeptical   8. despot   9. heretic   10. zealot   11. miser
12. bigoted   13. sycophant   14. verify

Rhyme Time (page 33)
1. Gluttony (Yes, Orson Welles really said this.)   2. fanatic
3. oracle   4. skeptic   5. sycophant   6. hedonist   7. inexorable
8. aver

Matching (page 34)
1. (m) Scrooge, (c) hoarder
2. (d) nonbeliever, (p) one who differs
3. (f) tyrant, (h) autocrat
4. (i) fake, fraud; (g) impostor
5. (a) bias, (k) prejudice
6. (o) confirm, (b) corroborate
7. (l) fanatical, (n) overeager
8. (j) one in revolt, (e) rebel

LIST 4
Fill in the Blanks (page 38)
1. superficiality   2. listlessness   3. fervor   4. profusion
5. vulnerability   6.indulgence   7. unobtrusiveness
8. uniformity

True or False (page 39)
1. T   2. F   3. F   4. T·   5. T   6. T   7. T   8. T   9. F
10. T

Matching Antonyms (page 40)
1. (a) irrelevant, (m) inappropriate
2. (d) restrained, (n) stingy
3. (e) inconsistent, (p) varied
4. (f) exhilarating, (k) restful
5. (g) thorough, (l) deeply serious
6. (b) weak, (q) ineffective
7. (j) critical, (o) unforgiving (maybe also n. *stingy*)
8. (h) bouncy, (s) enthusiastic
9. (i) gregarious, (r) friendly
10. (t) conspicuous, (c) aggressive

LIST 5
Matching (page 44)
1. (B) exceedingly particular, (C) meticulous
2. (C) disapprove of, (D) regret
3. (A) prideful, (D) overbearing
4. (A) stoop, (B) unbend
5. (B) scorn, (C) disdain
6. (C) belittle, (D) mock or jeer
7. (A) smug, (B) self-satisfied
8. (B) privilege, (D) right
9. (A) scoff at, (C) ridicule
10. (B) minimize, (C) decry

Words in Context (page 45)

1. openly and disdainfully proud
2. showy, self-important, pompous
3. disdainfully superior, scornful, proud
4. scorn, contempt
5. scorned, strongly disapproved of
6. scornful, disparaging, belittling, negatively critical
7. snootily and rather scornfully coming down to another's level (may be very subtle or quite open)
8. right, privilege
9. an "Oh, don't mind me" attitude that is modest and self-effacing, intended to put that person in the background
10. smugness, self-satisfaction

Analogies (page 46)

1. (D) Napoleon : arrogance :: Twain : satire
Person linked to well-known skill or trait.
2. (B) remark : disparaging :: attitude : scoffing
Implied comparison. A remark that puts another down is a *disparaging* remark, just as an attitude that puts another down is *scoffing*.
3. (D) pride : hauteur :: satisfaction : complacency
Escalating degree. Extreme pride is *hauteur* just as the extreme of satisfaction is *complacency*.
4. (E) derision : ridicule :: scorn : contempt
Analogy of definition or main characteristic. *Derision* always involves or means *ridicule*, just as *scorn* implies *contempt* (by definition).

REVIEW: LISTS 1–5
Find the Oddball (page 48)

1. heretic   2. hauteur   3. insist   4. nasty   5. hyperbole
6. interesting   7. provoke   8. inevitable   9. hedonist
10. hackneyed

True or False (page 49)

1. T   2. F   3. F   4. F   5. F   6. F   7. T   8. T   9. T
10. F

Find the Synonym (page 50)

1. equivocal   2. to concur   3. banal   4. listless   5. to chastise
6. charlatan   7. to condone   8. precursor   9. inexorable
10. grueling   11. profuse   12. potent

Who Said That? (page 51)

1. orator   2. raconteur   3. glutton   4. recluse   5. skeptic
6. despot   7. insurgent   8. scoffer (or *deprecator*)   9. heretic

10. equivocator   11. interrogator   12. deprecator

Matching (page 52)

1. to come together   2. to praise   3. superficial or hasty
4. pompous language   5. banality   6. to declare firmly
7. accidental   8. to ridicule   9. right or privilege
10. disdain, scorn   11. to increase   12. to scatter or fan out
13. to obliterate; wear away   14. lenient   15. continuous

LIST 6

Rhyme Time (page 56)
1. raze   2. immutable   3. posit   4. meander   5. mutant

Matching (page 56)
1. (A) blemish, (C) spoil
2. (C) relieve, (D) alleviate
3. (B) efface, (C) wipe out
4. (A) snub, (D) reject
5. (B) collect, (D) accumulate
6. (A) cloud over, (B) conceal
7. (C) study carefully, (D) examine
8. (B) wander, (C) ramble
9. (C) soothe, (D) appease
10. (B) tear down, (D) demolish
11. (A) invalidate, (D) negate
12. (B) mind or obey, (C) consider

Substitution (page 58)
1. heed   2. proponent   3. marred   4. obscured   5. mitigate
6. rebuffed   7. placate   8. perusing   9. nullify   10. garnered

LIST 7

Fill in the Blanks (page 63)
1. virtuosos or virtuosi   2. quandary   3. lucid   4. parsimonious
5. zenith   6. Torpor   7. nostalgia   8. volition   9. reticent
10. temerity

Matching Antonyms (page 64)
1. confidence   2. bombast   3. nadir   4. hyperactive
5. timidity   6. to obscure   7. order   8. beginner
9. descendant   10. generosity

Find the Oddball (page 65)
1. assortment   2. angle   3. niece   4. instinct   5. temperament
6. quest   7. betrayal   8. transparent   9. fear   10. quaintness

LIST 8

Find the Synonym (page 69)
1. formidable   2. profound   3. untenable   4. tenet   5. resilient
6. astute   7. meticulous   8. tenacious   9. alleviate

True or False (page 69)
1. F   2. T   3. F   4. T   5. T   6. F   7. T   8. T   9. T
10. F   11. F

Analogies (page 71)
1. **The correct answer is (C).** lawyer : astute :: pathologist : painstaking
Person linked to most desirable trait.
2. **The correct answer is (D).** profound : thoughtful :: sagacious : bright
Descending degree. *Profound* is deeply thoughtful just as *sagacious* is exceedingly bright.

3. The correct answer is (D). Supreme Court : sagacity ::
muscles : resilience
Noun linked to most critical quality, one that is the defining factor.
4. The correct answer is (E). formidable : defense :: redoubtable
: warrior
Noun linked to logical adjective. The best kind of defense is *formidable*, just as the best warrior is *redoubtable*.

LIST 9
Word Analysis *(page 75)*
1. good or mellow, jangly or jarring noise   **2.** optimist, pessimist
3. stringent, lax   **4.** Objective, subjective   **5.** concrete, abstract
6. burgeon, atrophy   **7.** affluent, indigent   **8.** levity, gravity
9. consecrated, desecrates   **10.** irrefutable, refuted
11. irresolute, resolute

Using the Words *(page 76)*
1. atrophy, burgeon   **2.** irrefutable, refutable
3. objective, subjective   **4.** desecrate, consecrate
5. abstract, concrete   **6.** lax, stringent   **7.** cacophony, euphony
8. optimism, pessimism   **9.** gravity, levity   **10.** resolute, irresolute

LIST 10
Fill in the Blanks *(page 80)*
1. irascible   **2.** rancor (perhaps *rue* or *malice*)   **3.** premonition
4. surreptitiously   **5.** tawdry   **6.** sullen   **7.** writhing
8. malice (or *rancor*)   **9.** taciturn   **10.** servile   **11.** malice
12. rue

Matching *(page 82)*
1. (h) self-reproach, (m) guilty unease
2. (k) forewarning, (f) foreboding
3. (a) slander, (n) defame
4. (l) quietly resentful, (p) lowering
5. (c) bitterness, (t) old enmity
6. (d) cheap, (s) gaudy
7. (e) secretive, (o) deceptive
8. (b) laconic, (q) silent
9. (g) subservient, (j) abject
10. (i) testy, (r) choleric

Rhyme Time *(page 83)*
1. writhe   **2.** rue   **3.** admonished   **4.** malice   **5.** mediocre
6. mediate

REVIEW: LISTS 6–10
Find the Synonym *(page 84)*
1. obscure   **2.** mitigate   **3.** immutable   **4.** respite
5. parsimonious   **6.** lucid   **7.** astute   **8.** abstract   **9.** burgeon
10. resolute   **11.** sacrilege   **12.** taciturn

Analogies *(page 85)*

1. The correct answer is (D). symphony : violins :: religion : tenets
Part of a whole. Violins are a significant part of any *symphony*, just as various *tenets* are part of any religion.

2. The correct answer is (B). energy : torpor :: government : anarchy
Opposites. Also, think of this sentence: Lacking energy, you have *torpor*; lacking government, you have *anarchy*.

3. The correct answer is (B). sin : remorseful :: mistake : rueful
Implied comparison. If you commit a sin you feel *remorseful*, just as making a mistake causes you to feel *rueful*.

4. The correct answer is (E). past : nostalgia :: future : optimism
Implied comparison. We typically view the past with *nostalgia*, just as we view the future with *optimism*. Choice (C) is weak because not everyone views the present with pessimism.

5. The correct answer is (C). mediate : sage :: elucidate : teacher
Specific person linked to one major function inherent in that position. A sage is well qualified to *mediate*, just as a teacher is well qualified to *elucidate*.

6. The correct answer is (C). battle : trepidation :: enemy : rancor
Implied comparison. We typically view a battle with *trepidation* just as we view an enemy with *rancor*.

Matching Antonyms *(page 86)*

1. heir   **2.** indigent   **3.** levity   **4.** lax   **5.** rigidity
6. malicious   **7.** irritate   **8.** scan   **9.** ignore   **10.** temerity
11. silly   **12.** even-tempered

Fill in the Blanks *(page 87)*

1. garner   **2.** meticulous   **3.** reticent   **4.** rebuffed
5. razed, obliterating   **6.** volition   **7.** quandary   **8.** irrefutable
9. proponents   **10.** virtuosos   **11.** tenacious   **12.** zenith

LIST 11
Substitution *(page 92)*

1. rejuvenate   **2.** vacillating   **3.** implying   **4.** temper
5. acclaim   **6.** venerate or revere   **7.** scrutinized   **8.** disclaim
9. sanctions, sanction (v.)   **10.** waived

Find the Oddball *(page 93)*

1. sponge   **2.** twist   **3.** flinch   **4.** dankness   **5.** implied
6. deter   **7.** urge   **8.** discourage   **9.** relegate   **10.** reject

True or False *(page 94)*

1. F   **2.** T   **3.** T   **4.** T   **5.** T   **6.** F   **7.** F   **8.** T

LIST 12
Fill in the Blanks *(page 98)*

1. criteria   **2.** delineate   **3.** dearth, prodigious (or *copious*)
4. minced   **5.** magnanimously

Matching *(page 98)*

1. (B) briefness, (D) conciseness
2. (C) outline, (D) portray accurately
3. (B) immense, (C) enormous

237

4. (A) scarcity, (C) paucity
5. (A) fleeting, (B) transient
6. (C) scanty, (D) skimpy
7. (B) unnecessary, (D) superfluous
8. (A) generous in spirit, (D) big-hearted

Words in Context (page 100)

1. any standard used for making judgments
2. a person of rank, power, or influence
3. fading fast, like vapor
4. in great and plentiful supply
5. very, very tiny
6. talk indirectly or in any confusing way; mincing words with someone is failing to be direct
7. briefness, succinctness
8. big-hearted, forgiving
9. unnecessary, superfluous
10. enormous, huge, impressive

Matching Antonyms (page 101)

1. enduring, long-lived
2. scanty, minuscule, also meager
3. plentiful amount, copious
4. superabundance, plentiful amount
5. tiny, minuscule, also meager

LIST 13

Matching (page 105)

1. unwanted or unneeded   **2.** unavoidable   **3.** opportunistic
4. strenuous   **5.** insanely idealistic   **6.** of doubtful authorship
7. commonplace   **8.** abominable, appalling

Fill in the Blanks (page 105)

1. predilection   **2.** eclectic   **3.** prodigal   **4.** legitimate
5. legislate   **6.** negligible   **7.** ironic   **8.** aesthetic

Analogies (page 106)

1. The correct answer is (D). daydreaming : quixotic :: cleaning house : mundane
Activity linked to most logical descriptive adjective.
2. The correct answer is (E). bad : heinous :: difficult : arduous
Escalating degree. Bad is much less awful than *heinous*, just as difficult is much less demanding than *arduous*.
3. The correct answer is (B). apocryphal : legend :: fictitious : fable
Logical literary description linked to literary genre. Both legends and fables are apt to be made up—fictitious.

Find the Antonym (page 107)

1. apocryphal   **2.** quixotic   **3.** avoidable   **4.** desired
5. significant   **6.** aversion   **7.** haphazard   **8.** noble
9. customary   **10.** mundane   **11.** parsimonious   **12.** impractical

238

LIST 14
Substitution (page 110)
1. rhetorical   **2.** garble   **3.** diatribe   **4.** satire   **5.** blasphemy
6. garrulous   **7.** jargon   **8.** indicted   **9.** tirade   **10.** slander

True or False (page 112)
1. T   **2.** F   **3.** F   **4.** T   **5.** T   **6.** F   **7.** T

Matching (page 113)
1. wordy, garrulous   **2.** defame, slander (or *dishonor* or *malign*)
3. fretful, petulant   **4.** corrosive, caustic   **5.** command, legal
order   **6.** questioning, curious   **7.** defame, dishonor (or *malign*)

LIST 15
Words in Context (page 116)
1. *indifferent* = unconcerned, aloof, unattached, uninterested
2. *capitulate* = yield or give in to what another wants
3. *defer* = put off until another time
4. *innocuous* = harmless
5. *languor* = sluggishness, lethargy
6. *stagnant* = stale, unmoving, inactive
7. *deduced* = concluded or inferred through reasoned thought

Matching (page 117)
1. (A) vary up or down, (D) come and go
2. (B) suspicious, (C) of doubtful quality
3. (C) wishy-washiness, (D) indecision
4. (A) hesitant, (B) unsure

5. (B) languorous, (D) torpid
6. (C) indefinite, (D) uncertain
7. (A) avoid, (C) circumvent
8. (B) promoting, (D) assisting
9. (C) permeate, (D) diffuse throughout

Find the Synonym (page 119)
1. evade   **2.** defer   **3.** languor   **4.** innocuous   **5.** stagnant
6. indifferent   **7.** tentative   **8.** capitulate

REVIEW: LISTS 11–15
Analogies (page 120)
1. The correct answer is (C). vacillate : ambivalence :: blaspheme : irreverence
Implied comparison. To *vacillate* is to reveal *ambivalence*, just as to *blaspheme* shows *irreverence*.

2. The correct answer is (D). ephemeral : duration :: meager : amount
Words of measurement in implied comparison. Something that is only *ephemeral* in duration won't last long, just as something *meager* in amount won't last very long either.

3. The correct answer is (B). satire : irony :: tirade : criticism
Part of a whole or related by definition, maybe even implied comparison! Think of this sentence: *Irony* is basic to *satire*, just as *criticism* is the basis of a *tirade*.

4. The correct answer is (E). reputation : slander :: communication : garble
Implied comparison. To *slander* a reputation ruins it, just as to *garble* a bit of communication ruins it.

239

5. The correct answer is (B). spirit : magnanimous :: effort : prodigious
Relationship of size. A big spirit is a *magnanimous* one, just as a big effort is a *prodigious* one.

Matching *(page 121)*
1. (B) give way to   **2.** (A) hint   **3.** (C) foil   **4.** (D) sharpen   **5.** (A) natural preference   **6.** (B) demanding   **7.** (B) fictitious   **8.** (D) languor   **9.** (C) beyond question   **10.** (A) superfluous

Find the Oddball *(page 122)*
1. announce   **2.** adjudicate   **3.** admonish   **4.** speech   **5.** jargon   **6.** dirty   **7.** menial   **8.** vapor   **9.** unreal   **10.** goal-oriented   **11.** supply   **12.** adorable

Fill in the Blanks *(page 123)*
1. waive   **2.** tentative   **3.** conducive   **4.** copious, prodigious   **5.** prodigal   **6.** eclectic   **7.** aesthetic   **8.** fluctuated, negligible   **9.** pervasive, deduced   **10.** vitriolic, vilified   **11.** diatribe, capitulated, innocuous   **12.** saturated, clamoring

LIST 16
Fill in the Blanks *(page 128)*
1. enjoins   **2.** undermined   **3.** extorting   **4.** solicitous   **5.** emanates   **6.** rescinded   **7.** extricate   **8.** emulate   **9.** expedite   **10.** subjugating   **11.** relegate   **12.** enhances

Rhyme Time *(page 130)*
1. repudiate   **2.** hamper, relegated   **3.** rescind, enhance   **4.** squander   **5.** extort

Matching *(page 131)*
1. facilitate   **2.** squander   **3.** ask for   **4.** hamper   **5.** weaken gradually   **6.** seep out   **7.** forbid   **8.** try to equal   **9.** tortuous   **10.** repeal

LIST 17
True or False *(page 135)*
1. F   **2.** T   **3.** T   **4.** F   **5.** T   **6.** F   **7.** F   **8.** T   **9.** T   **10.** T

Find the Oddball *(page 136)*
1. outlook   **2.** honor   **3.** urgency   **4.** symbiosis   **5.** master   **6.** hackneyed   **7.** aloof

Matching *(page 136)*
1. sloth, idleness   **2.** mercy, lenience   **3.** a cleansing, a purging   **4.** wrong assumption, error   **5.** obstacle, impediment   **6.** paradox, irregularity   **7.** neophyte, novice   **8.** convivial, sociable   **9.** original, new   **10.** outstandingly bad, flagrant

LIST 18
Find the Synonyms (page 141)
1. frivolity **2.** amiable **3.** jocular (*effervescent* is okay)
4. dispassionate **5.** apathetic **6.** effervescent **7.** serene
8. benign **9.** amity **10.** jocular

Fill in the Blanks (page 142)
1. benign or serene **2.** extolled **3.** placid **4.** effervescence
5. ameliorate **6.** frivolous **7.** Blithe **8.** assuage **9.** elation
10. blithe, amiable, or maybe jocular; appease

Find the Antonyms (page 143)
1. downcast **2.** effervescent **3.** irritate **4.** dispassionate
5. censure **6.** frivolous **7.** overwrought

LIST 19
Words in Context (page 147)
1. *unsavory* = unappetizing, unappealing, disgusting
2. *inflated* = puffed up, enlarged
3. *impotent* = powerless, ineffective
4. *partial* = biased, strongly disposed toward
5. *intangible* = not concrete, impalpable yet real
6. *auspicious* = favorable, boding well, propitious
7. *indiscriminate* = randomly, without discrimination
8. *dissent* = disagreement
9. *autocrat* = despot, tyrant, dictator
10. *aristocracy* = ruling class; qualified ones

True or False (page 148)
1. F **2.** T **3.** F **4.** F (maybe T!) **5.** T **6.** T (You can guess this one even if you don't know for sure.) **7.** T **8.** F
9. T **10.** T

LIST 20
Substitution (page 153)
1. didactic **2.** gullible **3.** incorrigible **4.** inane, wanton
5. tedious **6.** docile, pompous **7.** officious **8.** petty
9. dogmatic **10.** insipid

Matching (page 154)
1. inconstant, changeable **2.** naive, ingenuous **3.** dull, flavorless **4.** pedantic, preachy **5.** delinquent, recalcitrant
6. witless, insipid **7.** unchecked, inhumane **8.** established, traditional **9.** compliant, tractable **10.** interfering, impertinent

Find the Oddball (page 155)
1. ugly **2.** unsavory **3.** biased **4.** theoretical **5.** moderate
6. fickle

REVIEW: LISTS 16–20
Analogies (page 156)
1. The correct answer is (D). reasoning : fallacious :: judgment : biased
Implied comparison. The worst kind of reasoning would be *fallacious*, just as the worst kind of judgment would be *biased*.

241

2. The correct answer is (C). infamy : censure :: virtue : extol
Cause and effect. Historically, we *censure* infamy, just as we *extol* virtue.

3. The correct answer is (E). pleasant : jocular :: contented : blithe
Ascending degree.

4. The correct answer is (A). demagogue : sincerity :: neophyte : experience
Person and missing trait. A *demagogue* usually lacks sincerity, just as a *neophyte* lacks experience.

5. The correct answer is (B). effervescent : elation :: deflated : repudiation
Cause and effect. The result of elation is an *effervescent* feeling, just as the result of repudiation is a *deflated* feeling.

6. The correct answer is (E). confidence : undermine :: embankment : erode
Implied comparison. Confidence can be *undermined* in the same way that an embankment is *eroded*. (Very similar processes although one is concrete, the other abstract.)

Matching Antonyms (page 157)

1. concrete   2. humble   3. carefully controlled   4. hinder
5. aggravate   6. ominous, foreboding   7. agreement
8. engrossing, absorbing   9. ineffective   10. disgrace
11. similarity   12. implicate

Find Those Synonyms (page 158)

1. hinder, impede   2. repeal, call back   3. enjoin, command
4. tortuous, crooked   5. novice, beginner   6. gregarious, amicable   7. vacillating, inconstant   8. assuage, conciliate
9. unfeeling, apathetic   10. insipid, empty

Good Words Get Around (page 159)

1. undermining   2. impartial   3. squander   4. alleviates
5. placid   6. frivolous   7. dogmatic   8. petty

LIST 21
Fill in the Blanks (page 164)

1. credulous   2. scrupulous   3. Steadfast   4. thrifty, prudence
5. pragmatist   6. exemplary   7. frugality, diligence, prudence, discretion, and thrift, plus probably pragmatism and steadfastness, too—eight virtues in all!   8. parochial (narrow)   9. solemnity, solemn   10. credibility, generic

Add the Synonyms (page 165)

1. frugal, sparing, provident   2. prudent, also modest
3. parochial   4. exemplary   5. scrupulous   6. steadfast, faithful
7. congenial, with kindred tastes

True or False (page 165)

1. T   2. F   3. T   4. F (probably)   5. F   6. F   7. T   8. T

LIST 22
Substitution (page 170)
1. intercede **2.** oblivious **3.** cryptic or enigmatic
4. hypothetical **5.** chimerical **6.** esoteric **7.** karma
8. elusive **9.** eccentric, precedent **10.** chronic, utopia

True or False (page 171)
1. T **2.** T **3.** F **4.** F **5.** F **6.** F **7.** T

Matching (page 172)
1. without example, novel **2.** perceptive, a seer **3.** aberrational, odd **4.** undecipherable, enigmatic **5.** "out to lunch," clueless
6. intervene, mediate **7.** repetitive, long-lasting **8.** secondhand, substitutionary **9.** ideal, perfect **10.** fanciful, imaginary

LIST 23
Fill-in Chart (page 176)
1. *vindictive*; dic/dict = say; revengeful, *spiteful*
2. turbulent; turb = agitate; *seething, agitated*
3. *homogeneous*; homo = same, gen = kind; same or alike throughout
4. *animosity*; anim = spirit, soul; enmity, *hatred*
5. *haphazard*; hap = luck, chance; *unplanned, random*
6. *equanimity*; equ = equal, same; anim = spirit, soul; *evenness of disposition, balance*
7. virulent; virus = poison; *noted for fast, powerful, and often fatal progress (virulent disease)*
8. convivial; con = with; viv = life; *party-loving, lively*
9. *ubiquitous*; ubique = everywhere; everywhere, *omnipresent*
10. precocious; pre = before; coquere = cooked; *mentally ahead of schedule, prematurely bright*

Rhyme Time (page 176)
1. voluminous **2.** voracious, whimsical **3.** ubiquitous, "viable"
4. unimpeachable **5.** incongruous

Word Analysis (page 177)
1. precocious **2.** incongruous **3.** turbulent **4.** voracious
5. whimsical **6.** vindictive

LIST 24
Fill in the Blanks (page 181)
1. extenuating **2.** iconoclast **3.** unethical **4.** kindle
5. elaboration **6.** tacit **7.** insidious **8.** tenuous **9.** unscathed
10. propensity

Matching Antonyms (page 182)
1. honorable **2.** peripheral **3.** kindle **4.** elaborate
5. discord **6.** deter **7.** spoken **8.** precipitate **9.** careless
10. traditionalist

Matching *(page 183)*

1. caustic, highly critical   **2.** tendency, inclination   **3.** around the edge, auxiliary   **4.** lack of harmony, strife   **5.** barely perceptible, flimsy   **6.** discourage, inhibit   **7.** dangerously alluring, subtle **8.** model, admired example   **9.** impetuous, headlong **10.** persistent, most attentive

LIST 25
Substitution *(page 187)*

1. arbitrary   **2.** desultory   **3.** detrimental   **4.** flagrant **5.** resigned   **6.** sporadic   **7.** capricious   **8.** blatant **9.** inherently   **10.** incisive

True or False *(page 188)*

1. F   **2.** F   **3.** F   **4.** T   **5.** F   **6.** F

Matching *(page 189)*

1. logical, lucid   **2.** succinct, brief   **3.** roundabout, crafty **4.** agreeable, well-suited   **5.** liable, receptive to   **6.** irrelevant, nonessential   **7.** inborn, natural   **8.** "loud," glaring **9.** irregular, inconstant   **10.** despotic, impulsive

REVIEW: LISTS 21–25
Analogies *(page 190)*

1. The correct answer is (D). time : anachronistic :: setting : incongruous
Implied comparison. Something out of place in time is *anachro-*

nistic, just as something out of place in a particular setting appears *incongruous*: it "doesn't fit."

2. The correct answer is (B). prophet : clairvoyant :: paradigm : exemplary
Person related to most logical trait. A prophet should be *clairvoyant*, just as a paradigm should be ex*emplary*.

3. The correct answer is (D). apparent : flagrant :: careful : assiduous
Ascending degree. *Flagrant* is the extreme of apparent, just as *assiduous* is the extreme of careful.

4. The correct answer is (E). water : turbulent :: thought : incoherent
Implied comparison. Churning water is *turbulent*, just as churning thought is *incoherent*.

5. The correct answer is (B). appetite : voracious :: apparel : voluminous
Comparison of size. A big, impressive appetite is often termed *voracious*, just as noticeable clothing that billows about like sails on a ship is termed *voluminous*.

6. The correct answer is (A). extraneous : detail :: peripheral : issue
Comparison of location or function. An unnecessary detail is *extraneous*, just as an unnecessary issue is *peripheral*.

Find the Oddball *(page 191)*

1. brilliant (others related by the root *gen*)   **2.** prophecy **3.** pragmatic   **4.** running   **5.** hideous   **6.** fragile   **7.** elucidate **8.** alternate   **9.** erroneous   **10.** indigent   **11.** inspired **12.** reclusive

244

Who Said That? *(page 192)*

1. pious one   **2.** iconoclast   **3.** clairvoyant   **4.** eccentric
5. arbitrary one   **6.** pragmatist   **7.** credulous one   **8.** vindictive
one   **9.** convivial soul

Find the Synonyms *(page 193)*

1. congenial, compatible   **2.** capricious, whimsical   **3.** desultory,
haphazard   **4.** cryptic, enigmatic   **5.** frugal, thrifty
6. parochial, narrow   **7.** flimsy, tenuous   **8.** tacit, unspoken
9. propensity, tendency   **10.** chimerical, fanciful

The Root of It All *(page 194)*

1. ad*hes*ive   **2.** *genius*   **3.** in*genu*ous   **4.** *gene*   **5.** en*gen*der
6. *gen*eric   **7.** dis*ingenu*ous   **8.** *cred*ible   **9.** inter*cede*
10. *chron*ic   **11.** *anim*osity   **12.** equ*anim*ity   **13.** in*sid*ious
14. ex*ten*uating   **15.** in*cis*ors

LIST 26
Fill in the Blanks *(page 198)*

1. enervating, exhaust   **2.** belittle   **3.** carping   **4.** bolster
5. infer   **6.** perceptive   **7.** depleting (maybe *exhausting*)
8. incipient   **9.** facilitate   **10.** coercion, cajoled

Antonyms *(page 199)*

1. undermine   **2.** replenish   **3.** extol (also, *acclaim*)
4. terminal, final   **5.** hamper, hinder   **6.** dull, obtuse
7. energize   **8.** contain   **9.** acclaim (*extol* is okay)

Switcheroo *(page 200)*

1. estrangement   **2.** sponsorship, support   **3.** exhaustion
4. keenness   **5.** supporter   **6.** (rapid) multiplication
7. conclusion, deduction   **8.** negative criticism   **9.** wheedling,
begging   **10.** force

LIST 27
True or False *(page 204)*

1. F   **2.** F   **3.** T   **4.** T   **5.** T   **6.** T   **7.** T   **8.** F   **9.** T
10. T

Find the Synonyms *(page 205)*

1. fantastic, shocking   **2.** unimaginative, ordinary   **3.** ludicrous,
absurd   **4.** unchanging, stationary   **5.** sophisticated, suave
6. obtuse, dull-witted   **7.** very clever, insidious   **8.** dormant,
potential   **9.** inborn, inherent   **10.** frank, guileless

Substitution *(page 206)*

1. prosaic, bizarre (or *zany*)   **2.** urbane, opaque   **3.** candid, stoic,
acrimonious   **4.** static (slang usage)   **5.** zany, futile

LIST 28
Find the Oddball *(page 210)*

1. skillful   **2.** dangerous   **3.** charming   **4.** wary   **5.** pedestrian

Matching *(page 210)*

1. refractory, unruly   **2.** prudent, watchful   **3.** unassertive, hesitant   **4.** outmoded, passé   **5.** totally accurate, demanding   **6.** productive, fertile   **7.** unimaginative, ordinary   **8.** very noticeable, striking   **9.** unnecessary, wasteful

Fill in the Blanks *(page 211)*

1. quizzical   **2.** obsolete   **3.** unassailable   **4.** salutary   **5.** reprehensible   **6.** conspicuous (a literal term, from actual citations)   **7.** fluent   **8.** Rigorous   **9.** mellifluous   **10.** volatile

LIST 29
Fill in the Blanks *(page 216)*

1. demeanor   **2.** nonchalantly   **3.** authoritarian   **4.** perfidy   **5.** erratic   **6.** contrite   **7.** spurious   **8.** austere   **9.** altruism   **10.** conciliatory

Who Said That? *(page 217)*

1. an austere person   **2.** the provincial   **3.** the brusque type   **4.** an altruist   **5.** a partisan   **6.** an infidel   **7.** the authoritarian   **8.** a perfidious one   **9.** a nonchalant one

True or False *(page 218)*

1. T   **2.** F   **3.** T   **4.** T   **5.** F   **6.** T   **7.** T   **8.** F

LIST 30
Words in Context *(page 222)*

1. *clandestine* = secret, surreptitious; *furtive* = on the sly, secret; *apprehensive* = worried, fearful of something bad
2. *depraved* = morally corrupt; *deleterious* = injurious, harmful
3. *decadence* = decay of moral standards and ethical conduct
4. *caustic* = biting, cutting, corrosive; *cynic* = person who distrusts human nature and views people pessimistically
5. *crass* = lacking good taste, crude, vulgar
6. *guileless* = lacking guile or trickery, ingenuous, open
7. *rebellious* = stubbornly resistant to authority
8. *negligence* = lack of care and attention, neglect; *morosely* = sullenly, gloomily

Matching Synonyms *(page 223)*

1. secret   **2.** to go apart   **3.** biting, corrosive   **4.** different   **5.** foreboding   **6.** deterioration   **7.** in poor taste   **8.** spoiling for a fight   **9.** deceit   **10.** pessimistic

Rhyme Time *(page 223)*

1. morose   **2.** depravity   **3.** furtive   **4.** bellicose (maybe *belligerent*, but it has too many syllables)   **5.** diverged

REVIEW: LISTS 26–30
Analogies *(page 225)*

1. The correct answer is (D). document : spurious :: passport : false

246

Implied comparison. A fake document is often termed *spurious*, just as a fake passport is usually termed *false*.

2. The correct answer is (C). resources : deplete :: strength : exhaust

Implied comparison. To use up nearly all of your resources is to *deplete* them (common usage), just as using up nearly all of your strength is to *exhaust* it.

3. The correct answer is (E). carping : alienation :: negligence : decadence

Cause and effect. *Carping* (repeated criticism) often leads to alienation, just as negligence may lead to *decadence* (deterioration and decay).

4. The correct answer is (B). misanthrope : cynical :: stoic : impassive

Person and most logical trait.

5. The correct answer is (A). subtle : covert :: flagrant : conspicuous

Synonymous or by-definition relationship. Something *subtle* is by its nature a covert thing, just as something *flagrant* is bound to be conspicuous.

6. The correct answer is (B). partisan : aloof :: infidel : loyal

Person and least likely trait/missing trait. A *partisan* will never remain aloof, just as an *infidel* will not remain loyal (to whatever group he once belonged to).

Matching Antonyms *(page 226)*

1. laudable **2.** provincial **3.** guileful **4.** belittle **5.** deleterious **6.** docile **7.** learned, acquired **8.** self-indulgence **9.** vital **10.** conciliatory **11.** coerce **12.** self-absorption

Matching *(page 227)*

1. orally skilled, graceful **2.** potential, dormant **3.** unassertive, hesitant **4.** remorseful, repentant **5.** gross, tasteless **6.** surreptitious, clandestine **7.** perceptive, pointed **8.** conclude, deduce **9.** pedestrian, everyday **10.** autocratic, despotic

Fill in the Blanks *(page 228)*

1. prolific, diverse **2.** static **3.** facilitate, futile **4.** erratic, aberration **5.** circumspect **6.** morose, rigorous **7.** denouncing, caustic **8.** bellicose, advocate

True or False *(page 229)*

1. T **2.** F **3.** T **4.** T **5.** T **6.** F

INDEX OF WORDS AND ROOTS

The words and roots taught in this book are presented here in alphabetical order for ease of reference. Following each word is the number of the list in which it appears. Roots are in bold type.

incorrigible—20
indefatigable—8
indict—14
indifferent—15
indigent—9
indiscriminate—19
indoctrinate—20
indolence—17
indulgent—4
inevitable—13
inexorable—3
infamous—19
infer—26
infidel—29
inflate—19
inherent—25
innate—27
innocuous—15
innovate—17
inquisitive—14
insidious—24
insipid—20
insurgent—3
intangible—19
intercede—22
irascible—10
irony—13
irrefutable—9
irresolute—9

jargon—14
jeopardy—17
jocular—18
judicious—8
jug/junct/join—16

karma—22
kindle—24

laconic—2
lampoon—2
languor—15
latent—27
laud—1
lax—9
leg (law)—13
leg/lect/lig—13
legacy—13
legitimate—13
lethargy—15
lev—8
leverage—8
levity—9
listless—4
**loc/loqu/log/
  ology**—2
loquacious—2
lu/luc—7
lucid—7

magn—12
magnanimous—12
magnate—12
mal—A Quick
  Review
malice—10
malign—10
mar (verb)—6
mar (sea)—A
  Quick Review
mater—A Quick
  Review
meager—12
meander—6
medi—10
mediate—10
mediocre—10
mellifluous—28
meticulous—8
min—12
mince—12
minuscule—12
misanthrope—27
miser—3
miss/mit—1
mitigate—6
mon/monit—10
morose—30
mundane—13

mut/mutat—6
mutation—6

neg—A Quick
  Review
negligence—30
negligible—13
neophyte—17
neutral—19
nonchalant—29
nostalgia—7
nov/neo—17
novel—17
nullify—6

objective—9
obliterate—6
oblivious—22
obscure—6
obsolete—28
officious—20
omnipotent—4
opaque—27
optimism—9
ora—3
oracle—3
orthodox—20
overt—30

painstaking—8

pandemic—19
paradigm—24
parochial—21
parsimony—7
partial—19
partisan—29
pater—A Quick
  Review
path/pass—18
paucity—12
pedestrian—28
perceptive—26
perfidy—29
peripheral—24
peruse—6
pervade—15
pessimism—9
petty—20
philanthropy—27
phon—9
phonics—9
pious—21
plex/plic/ply—11
pon/pos—6
posit—6
placate—6
placid—18
platitude—2
pompous—20

pot/poss—4
potent—4, 19
pragmatic—21
precedent—22
precipitate—24
preclude—4
precocious—23
precursor—1
predecessor—7
predilection—13
premonition—10
prerogative—5
pretentious—5
prodigal—13
prodigious—12
profound—8
profuse—4
proliferate—26
prolific—28
propensity—24
proponent—6
prosaic—27
provincial—29
prudent—21

quandary—7
quer/quir/quis—14
querulous—14
quixotic—13
quizzical—28

251

FAVORITE TITLES FOR READING

Even if you're a rabid reader, you may not be familiar with some of the titles on this list, all named "great books" by young adults. Some of them are old, some are new, but all are beloved. So grab a soda, get some popcorn, and settle back, because reading is *by far* the best way to increase your vocabulary—and it's a lot more fun than studying a word list.

P.S. If the book says it's for ages 9 to 12, ignore that. The books listed here are for everybody!

GREAT STORIES = "GREAT READS"

Burns, Olive Ann	*Cold Sassy Tree*
Crutcher, Chris	*Staying Fat for Sarah Byrnes*
Dumas, Alexandre	*The Count of Monte Cristo; The Three Musketeers*
Frazier, Charles	*Cold Mountain*
Golden, Arthur	*Memoirs of a Geisha*
Hiassen, Carl	*Hoot*
Holland, Isabelle	*The Man Without A Face*
Hugo, Victor	*Les Miserables; The Hunchback of Notre Dame*
Hurston, Zora Neale	*Their Eyes Were Watching God*
Irving, John	*The Cider House Rules; A Prayer for Owen Meany*
Kidd, Sue Monk	*The Secret Life of Bees*
Kingsolver, Barbara	*Prodigal Summer; The Poisonwood Bible*
Kingston, Maxine Hong	*The Woman Warrior*
Lee, Harper	*To Kill A Mockingbird*
Levine, Gail Carson	*Dave at Night*
MacLean, Norman	*A River Runs Through It*
McCourt, Frank	*Angela's Ashes*
McCullough, Colleen	*The Thorn Birds*
Michener, James	*Hawaii; The Drifters; Caravans*

Mitchell, Margaret	*Gone With The Wind*
Morrison, Toni	*Sula*
Rand, Ayn	*The Fountainhead*; *Atlas Shrugged*
Tademy, Lalita	*Cane River*
Wells, Rebecca	*Little Altars Everywhere*; *Divine Secrets of the Ya-Ya Sisterhood*

ADVENTURE/SUSPENSE

Clavell, James	*Tai-Pan*; *Shogun*; *King Rat*
Crichton, Michael	*Jurassic Park*; *The Andromeda Strain*
Follett, Ken	*Eye of the Needle*; *The Key to Rebecca*; *The Man from St. Petersburg*; *On Wings of Eagles*
Forsyth, Frederick	*The Day of The Jackal*; *The Odessa File*
King, Stephen	*The Stand*; *Pet Sematary*; *Firestarter*
London, Jack	*The Call of the Wild*; *White Fang*; *The Sea Wolf*

Paulsen, Gary	*Hatchet*
Uris, Leon	*Exodus*; *Battle Cry*
Wouk, Herman	*The Caine Mutiny*; *The Winds of War*; *War and Remembrance*

FANTASY

Adams, Richard	*Watership Down*; *The Plague Dogs*
Jacques, Brian	*Mossflower*; *Redwall, etc.* (Series)
Levine, Gail Carson	*Ella Enchanted*; *The Wish*
Marquis, Don	*Archy and Mehitable*
Naylor, Phyllis Reynolds	*Sang Spell*; *Jade Green*
Rowling, J.K.	*Harry Potter* (Series)
Stewart, Mary	*The Crystal Cave*
Tolkien, J.R.	*The Hobbitt*; *The Lord of the Rings* (Trilogy)
White, T.H.	*The Once and Future King*
Wyndham, John	*The Day of the Triffids*

HUMOR

| Bryson, Bill | *A Walk in the Woods* |

Cuppy, Will	*The Decline and Fall of Practically Everybody*
Dennis, Patrick	*Auntie Mame*
Durrell, Gerald	*My Family and Other Animals*; *Birds, Beasts, and Relatives*
Edgerton, Clyde	*Walking Across Egypt*
Ephron, Nora	*Scribble, Scribble*
Grisham, John	*Skipping Christmas*
Herriot, James	*All Creatures Great and Small*
Kotzwinkle, William	*The Bear Went Over the Mountain*
MacDonald, Betty	*The Egg and I*; *The Plague and I*
Mayle, Peter	*A Year in Provence*
Mowat, Farley	*The Dog Who Wouldn't Be*; *Owls in the Family*
Plimpton, George	*Paper Lion*
Peck, Richard	*A Long Way From Chicago*; *A Year Down Yonder*
Russo, Richard	*Straight Man*
Twain, Mark	*The Adventures of Huckleberry Finn*

White, Bailey	*Mama Makes Up Her Mind*
Wouk, Herman	*Don't Stop The Carnival*; *Inside, Outside*

MYSTERIES

Christie, Agatha	*Murder on the Orient Express*; *Sparkling Cyanide*
Doyle, Arthur Conan	*Sherlock Holmes mysteries* (e.g., *The Hound of the Baskervilles*)
Duncan, Lois	*Stranger With My Face*
Grimes, Martha	*Help The Poor Struggler*; *The Old Silent*
James, P.D.	*Original Sin*; *Cover Her Face*
Hiassen, Carl	*Basket Case*; *Skin Tight*; *Stormy Weather*
Hillerman, Tony	*First Eagle*; *The Fallen Man*; *Skinwalkers*
Marsh, Ngaio	*Vintage Murder*; *Died in the Wool*
Pullman, Philip	*The Ruby in the Smoke* (Trilogy)

Sayers, Dorothy	*The Nine Tailors*
Tey, Josephine	*The Singing Sands*; *A Shilling for Candles*

NONFICTION

Armstrong, Lance	*It's Not About the Bike*
Bryson, Bill	*In a Sunburned Country*
Camuti, Dr. Louis J.	*All My Patients Are Under the Bed*
Cordingly, David	*Under the Black Flag*
Feynman, Richard	*Surely You're Joking, Mr. Feynman*
Hillenbrand, Laura	*Seabiscuit*

Horner, John K.	*Digging Dinosaurs*
Junger, Sebastian	*The Perfect Storm*
MacLean, Norman	*Young Men and Fire*
Mowat, Farley	*Never Cry Wolf*
North, Sterling	*Rascal*
Paulsen, Gary	*Winterdance*
Philbrick, Nathaniel	*In the Heart of the Sea*
Smith, Red	*The Red Smith Reader*
Steinbeck, John	*Travels With Charley*
Stevenson, William	*A Man Called Intrepid*
Warner, William	*Beautiful Swimmers*
Zinsser, William	*Spring Training*

NOTES

NOTES

NOTES

NOTES